Heaven. It's our home and where we belong. But do we know just what it is we look forward to? Derek Thomas shows us from God's word what we can expect in eternity. In doing so, he stirs a longing for the glories and joys to come. The question is, are you ready?

Christina Fox

Author of *A Heart Set Free* and *Closer Than a Sister*

Here is encouragement for us in a gloom-laden world where it is open season to discuss every once-taboo subject—with one notable exception: "What happens to me when I die?" In *Heaven on Earth* Dr. Derek Thomas draws on the teaching of the Bible to explain the Christian's unique answer. Always joyful, sometimes playful, he shows us what John Newton called the "Solid joys and lasting treasures" that are the Christian's birth-right. A truly hope-full, wonder-full, joy-full book to read, treasure, and share.

Sinclair B Ferguson

Associate Preacher, St Peter's Free Church, Dundee

We belong to a generation that is obsessed with the present. Not only that, but one that thinks little, if anything, of death and what lies beyond. But the greater tragedy is that too many Christians have embraced this same mentality. Ours is a generation dangerously unready for death and where it leads.

Derek Thomas has done us all a huge service in packing so much rich Bible teaching on this subject into so few pages. More than that, he has done so with all the warmth, humor and pastoral care that has marked his ministry from its very inception. A ministry that has provided comfort and hope to the dying and those who mourn the loss of loved ones for as long as I have known him. Since it addresses the one great certainty confronting every human being, it is a book that every one of us should read.

Mark G Johnston
Minister, Bethel Presbyterian Church, Cardiff

According to Dr. Derek W. H. Thomas, there will be dogs in heaven! But, and so far more importantly, the Lamb will be there. Confusion, uncertainty, anxiety—not to mention reams of false teaching—abound about heaven. Here a skillful pastor-theologian draws our eyes to Scripture's vision of our eternal home, the New Heaven and the New Earth. He also draws our attention to our eternal vocation, worshipping and adoring the Lamb. This book brims with hope, joy, and confidence.

Stephen J. Nichols
President, Reformation Bible College and Chief Academic officer,
Ligonier Ministries, Sanford, Florida

I have been reading Derek Thomas, and listening to him preach, for thirty years. He has a singular way of blessing God's people with God's word. I always come away wanting to be a better preacher, but above all, with clearer views of our great Savior, the Lord Jesus Christ. This book's topic, Heaven, is vital for the Christian life. Christians need to be clear on their hope, and we won't be clear on our hope until we take into our hearts a confident trust in what God in the Scriptures says is to come for all who trust in Christ. Take up and read then, and hope.

Ligon Duncan
Chancellor and CEO, Reformed Theological Seminary, Jackson, Mississippi

Sooner or later, almost every Christian has questions about heaven. What is it like? What happens when I die? What takes places at the end of human history? No one can avoid these questions, which is why I am grateful for this new book. As a faithful pastor, scholar, and student of the word, Derek Thomas makes for a terrific guide in exploring these critical matters. I was greatly edified in reading this book. You will be too.

Kevin DeYoung
Senior Pastor, Christ Covenant Church, Matthews, North Carolina, and Assistant Professor of Systematic Theology, Reformed Theological Seminary, Charlotte, North Carolina

We live in an age of mass confusion when it comes to death and the afterlife. Regrettably, even many within the church have adopted unbiblical notions with regard to heaven and hell. This book is a welcome resource for both pastors and lay people as they consider what the Bible says about what happens after we die. Derek Thomas is a careful, clear, and compelling biblical expositor. This is a pastoral and lucid treatment of heaven, hell, and the return of Christ that is firmly rooted in the biblical text. *Heaven on Earth* will make you long for the gift of eternal life with Christ and the hope of the resurrection.

Albert Mohler

Jr. President of the Southern Baptist Theological Seminary

Christians spend so much time fixing our eyes on our circumstances, instead of fixing our eyes on Jesus. As a result, many live fearful, anxious, and discouraged, unsure how and where to fix our eyes and find the hope only Jesus brings. Derek Thomas has provided the powerful answer in this book you hold in your hands. In *Heaven on Earth*, we are given that tangible place to look as we struggle in this fallen, broken world—heaven. Thomas has served every follower of Jesus with this well-written, beautiful, and biblical picture of heaven that will provide the God-given comfort we all need and seek. Every Christian needs to read this book!

Brian Croft

Senior Pastor, Auburndale Baptist Church

Founder of Practical Shepherding

Senior Fellow, Church Revitalization Center, Southern Baptist Theological Seminary

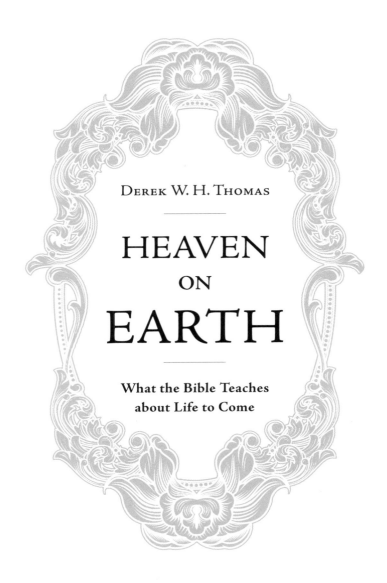

DEREK W. H. THOMAS

HEAVEN
ON
EARTH

What the Bible Teaches
about Life to Come

CHRISTIAN
FOCUS

Copyright © Derek W. H. Thomas 2018

paperback ISBN 978-1-52710-145-6
epub ISBN 978-1-5271-0146-3
mobi ISBN 978-1-5271-0147-0

10 9 8 7 6 5 4 3 2 1

Published in 2018
by
Christian Focus Publications, Ltd.
Geanies House, Fearn,
Ross-shire, IV20 1TW, Scotland
www.christianfocus.com

Cover design
by
Paul Lewis

Printed and bound by Bell & Bain, Glasgow

CONTENTS

To
Ralph & Barbara Davis
Grateful beyond words for your ministry

Introduction

Why a book about heaven?

For all the skepticism that abounds in our time, people still want to know what happens after death. Books and movies suggesting "post-mortem" experiences of "heaven" are wildly popular. Christians who should know better often cite these sources with approval, despite the often bizarre aspects of what they relate.

And what exactly do we mean when we talk about "heaven"? Are we talking about a conscious existence ten seconds after we are declared dead? Are we talking about what theologians refer to as "the intermediate state"? Or, are we talking about the final state of things, post-resurrection and all the other events that may or may not occur before or after the Second Coming, what the Bible refers to as "the new heaven and new earth"? These are two different places. I am persuaded that I shall be in heaven when I die; but I shall not spend eternity in *this* heaven. At the Resurrection, I shall live in the new heaven and new earth, with the emphasis on the new *earth*.

All the chapters in this book were preached as sermons before they emerged in written form. And preaching about what happens after death confirmed in me once again the vital importance of what happens *before* death. For, apart from the gospel—faith *alone* in Jesus Christ *alone*, apart from any works on our part—it is not heaven (in either sense) that awaits us, but everlasting punishment in hell. For that is what Jesus teaches, Jesus more than any other person in the Bible. To be assured of heaven, you must first believe the gospel, and commit to it *here and now* before we pass from this world into the next. It is my prayer, therefore, that readers of this book—whoever you may be—will ensure that they get right with God, before it is too late. Only then can heaven be entertained as an assurance and certainty.

I am grateful to William MacKenzie for suggesting that I write this book. The idea took hold on a delightful retreat to Limerick—not the one in Ireland, but the one near the South Carolina coastline—hosted by dear friends, Ken and Kathy Wingate. Also present on this occasion was my friend and colleague, Dale Ralph Davis and his wife, Barbara. In 2013, Dr. Davis agreed to my urgings that he move to Columbia with his wife and be the "evening preacher" at First Presbyterian Church. Imagine my surprise and delight when he agreed to do so! It has been a treasure beyond words to have sat under his unique and insightful preaching. I have sometimes thought that I would cross an ocean or two to hear him. But I don't have to. I just need to attend Sunday evening church! By way of a small token of my gratitude, I dedicate this book to him and his gracious wife, Barbara.

Derek Thomas

Columbia, South Carolina

2017

Chapter 1
We Die … Then what?

The boast of heraldry, the pomp of pow'r,
And all that beauty, all that wealth e'er gave,
Awaits alike th' inevitable hour.
The paths of glory lead but to the grave.
—Thomas Gray, *Elegy Written in an English Churchyard*

I have seen death occur many times. Life seems to disappear and suddenly there is only the faint recognition of the one we love. Changes occur in death. Blood ebbs away from the surface, muscles relax and the people we know don't quite look the same anymore.

The process that brings us to this point varies. For some, it is sudden. For others, it is the culmination of a long and often painful struggle against disease. But at some point, life ceases. Breathing stops. The pulse of a heart is heard no more. Brainwaves fail to reflect consciousness. Death has occurred.

And something always seems to be missing. Missing from their faces. It is the same person, but life has gone. The stillness of the body may appear eerie to those unacquainted with death. But it is the sight of the face that grips us most of all. Something has gone. Disappeared. The energy, the communication, that which made them uniquely who they were, isn't there anymore.

Where did that life go? The motionless body is there before us, but where is the one that we love? Where did consciousness go? Self-determination, drive, anticipation, aspirations... where are they? Are we simply a product of biological tissue and chemical interactions? Is that all there is to life? Is physiology the total explanation of all that we are? Is there life *after* death?

HOME AND AWAY

If there is no life after death, the issue is all too clear. She is nowhere. He no longer exists. The body that appears now like a shell, is still present (and let's assume for now that it is). There is no speech, no smile, no recognition, no longing, no creativity. There is no consciousness of themselves or us.

But is that really what happens? Consciousness ceases to exist?

Christians see it all very differently. Believers who have died are in another realm. She is in heaven. He is with Jesus.

... We know that while we are at home in the body we are away from the Lord, for we walk by faith, not by sight. Yes, we are of good courage, and we would rather be away from the body and at home with the Lord. (2 Cor. 5:6–8)

How can those who have died be "at home with the Lord"? Because there is more to us than our body. We are also soulish creatures. In brief, we are *ensouled*-bodies. That is, we are comprised of both a body and a soul. When the body ceases to live, we, our consciousness, our *soulish* part, continue to exist. We never really cease to exist. We simply continue in another realm of God's created order, in that realm where Jesus lives in His resurrected, ascended body.

Typically, we call this place, this existence, *heaven.*

At the very moment of death, Christians believe they go to heaven.

Immediately.

FIVE MINUTES AFTER DEATH

Do you know with any certainty what will happen to *you* when you die?

Let's be a little more specific. Where will *you* be, five minutes after you have been declared dead? Where will the conscious, thinking, self-aware, communicative you be?

We are asking more than a question about memory or influence. Nero, Augustine, and "Wild Bill" Hickok continue to exert an influence on us, even though all three have been dead a very long time. We are instead asking about self-awareness and creativity, features that identify that we are alive. What happens to these when our body is declared dead? And Christians have an answer that is certain and clear. Consciousness and all that goes with it continues in another realm, where Jesus exists in bodily form. And this place is called *heaven*.

When the New Testament addresses the issue of life after death, it often has in mind a more ultimate question: where will we spend *eternity*? Indeed, the focus of the New Testament is the resurrection body and the life that is to occur after Jesus returns to gather His people. Typical of such a focus is the great burden of 1 Corinthians 15:52–55:

> … *in a moment, in the twinkling of an eye, at the last trumpet. For the trumpet will sound, and the dead will be raised imperishable, and we shall be changed. For this perishable body must put on the imperishable, and this mortal body must put on immortality. When the perishable puts on the imperishable, and the mortal puts on immortality, then shall come to pass the saying that is written:*
>
> *"Death is swallowed up in victory."*
>
> *"O death, where is your victory?*
> *O death, where is your sting?"*

At the resurrection, our physical bodies will be renewed and reunited with our souls. After Jesus returns, our souls will be *embodied* again. This raises more questions, of course. Questions about what life is like *without a body*, and what kind of body are we to expect in the end? And will it be in any way recognizable, to us as well as to others? But we are ten steps ahead of ourselves.

Let's return to the point of departure from this present existence, the time of our death, and what immediately follows. What will the nature of our existence after death be like? Scripture has given us some clues.

A Story with a Sting in its Tale

Jesus tells a parable about two men, one rich and another poor. These two men have very different lives and very different destinies. The point of the story is clear: there is a heaven to be gained and a hell to be shunned, and the time to choose between these destinies is *now*.

There was a rich man who was clothed in purple and fine linen and who feasted sumptuously every day. And at his gate was laid a poor man named Lazarus, covered with sores, who desired to be fed with what fell from the rich man's table. Moreover, even the dogs came and licked his sores. The poor man died and was carried by the angels to Abraham's side. The rich man also died and was buried, and in Hades, being in torment, he lifted up his eyes and saw Abraham far off and Lazarus at his side. And he called out, "Father Abraham, have mercy on me, and send Lazarus to dip the end of his finger in water and cool my tongue, for I am in anguish in this flame." But Abraham said, "Child, remember that you in your lifetime received your good things, and Lazarus in like manner bad things; but now he is comforted here, and you are in anguish. And besides all this, between us and you a great chasm has been fixed, in order that those who would pass from here to you may not be able, and none may cross from there to us." And he said, "Then I beg you, father, to send him to my father's house—for I have five brothers—so that he may warn them, lest they also come into this place of torment." But Abraham said, "They have Moses and the Prophets; let them hear them." And he said, "No, father Abraham, but if someone goes to them from the dead, they will repent." He said to him, "If they do not hear Moses and the Prophets, neither will they be convinced if someone should rise from the dead." (Luke 16:19–31)

Two contrasting individuals. One is rich, very rich or "filthy" rich as we sometimes say. He wore purple cloth made from a dye extracted from snails (an expensive and difficult process) and undergarments made from the finest linen.

This is not a tale condemning wealth. Both Job and Abraham, two godly men in the Old Testament, were very wealthy. But with wealth comes responsibility and temptation and thus Jesus' warning, "hardly shall they who have riches enter the kingdom of God," adding that it would be easier for a camel to enter the eye of a needle than for a rich man to enter the kingdom of God (Matt. 19:24; Mark 10:25; Luke 18:25).

In the parable, the rich man is thoughtless, lacking basic concern for those in need. He uses his wealth ostentatiously. Every day, as he leaves his house, he sees

Lazarus but ignores him. He doesn't offer him food or fresh clothes. Nor does he offer help of any kind. He does not instruct his servants to provide Lazarus with the left-overs from his kitchen.

The rich man in the parable has no name. And in a Jewish culture, this is tragic. Traditionally, he is referred to as Dives, a word that stems from the Latin (Vulgate) translation for "rich". Calling him Dives detracts from the point of the original parable where he has no name, which *is* the point. He may be honored and applauded in the world, but in this story, he has no honor. In showing no mercy or pity to those less favored than himself, he does not deserve a name.

There is something indescribably sad when all that can be said about someone is, "She was rich," "He was well-off." No mention is made of great achievements in philanthropy, patriotism or love of community. Here is a self-centered man whose only concern is to advance himself.

LIFE ON THE OTHER SIDE OF THE TRACKS

And then there's Lazarus. A poor man. Someone who lives in utter destitution. Without the means to feed himself or acquire basic healthcare. Every day someone drops[1] him outside the rich man's house. And every day the rich man sees him and passes by without so much as a gesture of acknowledgment.

Like so many individuals living on the streets, the only companionship Lazarus has is a dog. And lest we

---

1   The Greek suggests he was "thrown."

sentimentalize this detail, the point is to emphasize his dehumanization. Lazarus is on the edge of life, barely able to survive from day to day.

But Lazarus has something that the rich man does not. He has a name—*Lazarus*!

He is not the Lazarus mentioned in the gospels, brother to Mary and Martha, whom Jesus raised from the dead. Lazarus was a fairly common name, derived from the Hebrew, "Eleazar" (which means, "God has helped").

As in life, so in death, these two men live and die on opposite sides of the track. Lazarus is carried by angels to Abraham's side (Luke 16:22). In contrast, the rich man finds himself in "Hades," a place of "torment" (Luke 16:23).

PARABLES—HOW SIGNIFICANT ARE THE DETAILS?

Before we proceed any further, we need to ask some basic questions about how we should interpret parables. A recent and popular view is that a parable *only has one main point*. The details should not be pressed into service. They are there merely for decoration purposes.

This point of view seems too simplistic. There are many details in this parable. What, for example, are we to make of the fact that both the rich man and Lazarus are described as having bodies subsequent to their death? Since the rich man's brothers are still alive, this is not depicting the final end of the world state of things, but the intermediate state. Are we to conclude that we can expect to have physical bodies in the intermediate state? Furthermore, since the rich man asks for Lazarus to come to him, are we to conclude that such a journey from heaven to Hades is possible? And are we further to conclude that upon death angels carry us into the presence of Abraham?

Clearly, at some point, the details are not meant to be pressed too far. A parable is an earthly story with a heavenly meaning. Parables function in much the same way as metaphors function. Thus, "the sun rises and falls" is understood to mean dawn and dusk, rather than a scientific description of a geocentric universe. *Some* of the details of a parable are there for effect rather than to provide us with doctrinal formulation.

But *something* in the parable must be true. True in the sense that a doctrine can be extracted from it, else it serves no real purpose.

Consciousness after Death

The parable assumes consciousness after death, both of the lost and saved.

Therefore, the parable rules out the notion of *soul-sleep,* the view that the soul is unconscious at the time of death. It also negates the idea that unbelievers cease to exist after death (some forms of annihilationism teach this point of view). Variations on these views arise in many forms and for different philosophical reasons. Secular materialists deny that anything *exists* after death or any time subsequent to death. Seventh Day Adventists and Jehovah Witnesses teach a form of soul-sleep (denying consciousness) in the interval between death and resurrection (though there are slight differences). And there are others who advocate the annihilation of the *lost* at the time of death while equally advocating the continued conscious existence of the saved. Clearly, Jesus tells a parable that suggests conscious life after death, on the part of unbelievers as well as the faithful.

Three significant New Testament passages address the issue of consciousness and (for believers) blessing immediately after death.

Jesus spoke to a penitent thief on the cross, and said: "… Truly, I say to you, today you will be with me in paradise." (Luke 23:43). The word "paradise" occurs in two other places in the New Testament. In 2 Corinthians, Paul speaks of a time when he was caught up to the "third heaven" (2 Cor. 12:2). Paul experienced it while he was still alive, of course. It wasn't clear to him whether the experience took place "in the body" or "out of the body." And there were aspects of it that he did not feel free to pass on. But the essence of paradise was being in the presence of Jesus. In Revelation 2:7, mention is given of the Tree of Life which is in the paradise of God, a reference to the final state rather than the intermediate state. The Tree of Life is in the middle of the New Jerusalem, in front of the throne where Jesus sits (Rev. 22:1–5). The dying thief is promised a *conscious* experience of paradise *immediately following his death.*

The second significant passage is when Paul expresses his difficulty in deciding whether being released from prison in Rome was preferable to being martyred: "to die is gain" and "to depart [is] to be with Christ" (Phil. 1:21, 23). Death brings the believer into a conscious and better experience of fellowship with Jesus.

The third passage is one we referred to earlier in this chapter:

> *So we are always of good courage. We know that while we are at home in the body we are away from the Lord, for we walk by faith, not by sight. Yes, we are of good courage, and we would rather be away from the body and at home with the Lord.* (2 Cor. 5:6–8)

Death ("away from the body") brings the believer into the immediate presence of Jesus as he now exists in his resurrection body ("at home with the Lord").

All three passages confirm the point of the parable of the rich man and Lazarus that we will be very much alive after we die.

THE GREAT GULF

In the parable, the rich man ends up in Hades. What exactly does the Bible mean by Hades? Some translations inaccurately employ the term "hell" instead of Hades. Hades is the Greek word for the Hebrew: "*Sheol*", a word used generally as a synonym for conscious existence and awareness after death, for both believers and unbelievers. Both experience an existence after death. In Acts 2:27, for example, Peter cites Psalm 16:10, "For you will not abandon my soul to Hades, or let your Holy One see corruption", using the Greek "*Hades*" for "*Sheol*". Peter is arguing that this Old Testament passage was a prediction of the resurrection of Jesus!

But make no mistake, Hades leads to hell for the wicked.

Without Jesus, the experience of death and what follows is a lonely one. The only relief for the rich man is for Lazarus to come and help him. Where are the rich man's friends? Speaking of hell rather than Hades, T. S. Eliot wrote in his play, *The Cocktail Party*:

> *What is hell? Hell is oneself.*
> *Hell is alone, the other figures in it*
> *Merely projections. There is nothing to escape from*
> *And nothing to escape to. One is always alone.*[2]

Can those who are in Hades find a way to heaven? If the rich man thinks that Lazarus can come to him, is it also possible that he can go and join Lazarus? C. S. Lewis, for example, imagined in his book *The Great Divorce*, a bus full of people on a journey from hell (or more accurately, Hades) to heaven. The image suggests some form of purgatory, a temporary habitation from which there is a way of escape. The Bible teaches no such view. There is no highway from Hades to heaven. Despite the rich man's plea for Lazarus to come to him, the point is made clear: "… between us and you a great chasm has been fixed, in order that those who would pass from here to you may not do so, and none may cross from there to us" (Luke 16:26).

"None may cross from there to us." There is a finality to these words. There is no evangelism after death. Where we

---

2   T. S. Eliot, *The Cocktail Party*, Act 1.

find ourselves after death is where we will be forever. What we are *in this life* determines whether we will be in heaven or Hades (or ultimately, hell).

How did the rich man end up here? He had no faith and no deeds that issue from faith. Selfishness and greed were the sum of his achievements. His life had been devoted to serving himself through the acquisition of wealth. He had used his wealth for personal ends. And Jesus tells a story with a sting in its tale. If you love your riches more than you love God, you may well end up in the same place as the rich man in this parable. If money matters more than people, it shows you have an unregenerate heart.

If Lazarus can't come to the rich man, can Lazarus be sent to the rich man's (living) brothers instead?

I AM MY BROTHER'S KEEPER

There is an understandable urgency about this second request. And Jesus' response in the parable is at once surprising and terrifying: they have the Bible! And if they don't believe the Bible, neither will they believe if someone is raised from the dead.

Ask yourself this: which would you think is more powerful as a testimony to the reality and truthfulness of the gospel, meeting someone who has risen from the dead or a Bible? Anyone who suggests that meeting someone who has been dead for several years would not be a powerful corroboration of the truth of Scripture is being disingenuous. Seeing a resurrection, or even seeing someone *after* a resurrection as people in the Bible saw

Jesus *after* He was raised from dead, must be one of the most extraordinary things ever! If I was given the choice of being there when Jesus appeared out of the tomb, or being given a brand new study Bible in real calf leather, I would choose ... well, never mind. The point is clear, if staggering. All the evidence we need to validate that there is a heaven to be gained and a hell to be shunned is to be found in Scripture, God's breathed-out word (2 Tim. 3:16–17). If we fail to listen to the Bible, we are not going to be impressed (in the right sense) by signs and wonders.

Peter makes the same point in one of his letters. He is talking about the time when Jesus was transfigured on the mountain. The three disciples, Peter, James and John saw something of Jesus' glory. They also heard the voice of the heavenly Father saying to His Son, "... This is my beloved Son, with whom I am well pleased." Peter goes on to say, "... we ourselves heard this very voice borne from heaven, for we were with him on the holy mountain" (2 Pet. 1:17–18).

Peter heard the voice of God! And then he adds this: "... we have the prophetic word more fully confirmed" (v. 19). Peter is telling us that a Bible (in his case the Old Testament and whatever parts of the New Testament were in existence) was more sure than hearing the voice of God on the Mountain of Transfiguration.

It is quite breathtaking in its implication. Few things could more powerfully illustrate that Scripture is God's Word written. And with the illuminating work of the Holy Spirit, Scripture is all we need to understand about life here in this world and life beyond the grave.

Do you want certainty that heaven and hell exist? The Bible insists upon it.

Do you want certainty as to where you will be when you die? The Bible provides it.

When a jailor, on the verge of suicide, asked how he could be saved and thereby be certain of heaven, Paul replied, "... Believe in the Lord Jesus, and you will be saved, you and your household" (Acts 16:31).

It is the only answer you need.

Chapter 2
Are You Ready?

And nothing can we call our own but death
And that small model of the barren earth
Which serves as paste and cover to our bones.
—Shakespeare: Richard II, Act 3, Scene ii

"Are you ready?"
"Ready for what?"
"Ready for heaven!"

That was the conversation we heard in the first chapter. Now we take it up again from a slightly different angle. To be ready for heaven we need to be ready to die.

The story is told of the seventeenth century puritan Thomas Goodwin, president of Magdalen College, Oxford. In the darkness of his study Goodwin was introduced to a prospective student, probably in his early teens. "Are you ready to die?" the president asked, at which point the young man fled. If, indeed, the story is true, Goodwin was asking a proper pastoral question, one that all should consider. Being ready to die is the greatest wisdom we can learn.

The apostle Paul told the church in Philippi that he was ready to die. "... My desire is to depart and be with Christ ..." (Phil. 1:23). He was in prison in Rome when he wrote these words. They are not the sentiments of a tired old man who has lost the will to live. Even though he lived several more years, Paul was ready to die. He knew what happens when Christians die. We might even say that he had a "homesickness" for heaven.

Homesickness? Yes, this is the right word, I think. One theologian put it precisely this way: "Our greatest affliction is not anxiety, or even guilt, but rather homesickness—a nostalgia or ineradicable yearning to be at home with God."[1]

We were made for something better, something more enduring than this world. Don't get me wrong, this world has its beauty and grandeur. As I write these words, a week has passed since a full solar eclipse in my home city. I had not seen one before. It was breathtaking and awesome. At totality, when everything became darker and even the crickets started chirping, I felt something of what the Psalmist meant when he cried, "The heavens declare the

---

1   Donald Bloesch, *Theological Notebook* (Colorado Springs, CO: Helmers and Howard, 1989), p. 183.

glory of God, and the sky above proclaims his handiwork" (Ps. 19:1). No man-made object could ever accomplish such a display of glory.

But this world is ugly, too. Floods and tornados, drought and scorching, life-destroying heat and, as I write, the impending threat of a category-5 hurricane. Not to mention poverty and crime and evil.

Everything we see and touch does not turn to gold. Moth and rust decays (cf. Matt. 6:19–20). Our world is out of joint, turned in upon itself, in pain and agony as if "waiting ... with eager longing for the revealing of the sons of God" (Rom. 8:19). Our world is "subjected to futility" (Rom. 8:20). Changing the metaphor, "... the whole creation has been groaning together in the pains of childbirth ..." (Rom. 8:22). It is as though the world about us is saying, "there's something better than this." And not just the world about us; the world within us echoes the same sentiment. All our striving and longing and yearning points to an existence that transcends the brokenness of our present lives.

God created us to reflect something of His image. Restored as this image is by spiritual rebirth, aspects of it remain "a work in progress." Christians live in a state of tension: the good, we do not; the evil, we do (Rom. 7:19). We hobble through life, sensing now and then the ages to come like glimpses of the sun on a cloudy day. Adopted as "sons of God," there are times when it appears life could not be better; but it can. What we *shall* be has not yet appeared (1 John 3:2). We find ourselves looking over the fence, longing for the day when sin and temptation no longer trouble us. We find ourselves longing for heaven. But the journey is as important as the destination.

Living Each Day as if it Were Our Last

Thomas Ken (1637–1711), whom Charles II appointed chaplain to the Princess Mary, wife of William of Orange, was a prolific hymn writer. One of his most well-known compositions is, "Awake my soul, and with the sun." The second verse contains these lines:

> *Thy precious time misspent, redeem,*
> *Each present day thy last esteem,*
> *Improve thy talent with due care;*
> *For the great day thyself prepare.*

Living each day as if our last. It sounds somewhat morbid, perhaps. But Christians know where they are going. And since we don't know when that transition will be, preparing for it and holding out the possibility that it might be sooner rather than later, seems a wise way to live.

In Psalm 90, Moses (the author of the psalm) stares death in the face. He contemplates the meaning of life and death and everything in between. The psalm's main point is to teach us "to number our days," and to remember (for we are prone to forget) that we will not live forever in this world. If we make it to seventy or perhaps eighty, it will be tough going and aging is not for wimps. His point is *not* that we should wish this life over; rather, knowing this

life's relative brevity, we should live our lives for God, and
"... get a heart of wisdom" (Ps. 90:12).

Should Christians wish their lives away? No, absolutely
not! We have a mandate to live our lives on earth to the
full, finding every opportunity to give glory to God in
the tasks He has given us, small and great. Paul's advice
is crystal clear: "... whether you eat or drink, or whatever
you do, do all to the glory of God" (1 Cor. 10:31). We are
to be steadfast, "... always abounding in the work of the
Lord ..." (1 Cor. 15:58).

Nevertheless, a tension exists. We have a calling from
God to live our lives here and now to the full, finding every
opportunity to serve Him and enjoy the good things He
gives us. But sometimes a desire for something more arises.
And when this world becomes too painful to endure, that
longing can be overwhelming. It is what Paul expressed
to the Philippians: "... My desire is to depart and be with
Christ ..." (Phil. 1:23). Paul was homesick for heaven.

HOMESICKNESS

Homesickness can be painful. My father was not a traveler.
He disliked being away from home. Indeed, his father (my
grandfather) once proudly told me that the furthest he had
ever travelled from home was Aberystwyth—a town that
was exactly thirty-eight miles away. He lived in the same
house for over ninety years and only traveled thirty-eight
miles!

My father inherited some of this fear of being away from
home. Once, to attend a family event, we traveled by train

to London. We had intended to spend a few days seeing the sights of this great city. But on the second morning he came down for breakfast and said he wished to go home. And I traveled with him. Rarely have I witnessed such excitement as my father's when he saw his home at the end of the lane. We had been gone less than forty-eight hours.

Homesickness is a reality and Christians know it well. There are times when circumstances are so difficult that heaven seems the better option.

Imagine, for example, a person who has been diagnosed with a virulent form of cancer. All treatment options have been exhausted. Mitigating the pain is the best that can be offered. How then should we pray? Imagine a pastor, at the bedside, with an anxious spouse and children waiting for him to pray. Barring some sort of miracle (and we must never rule out that possibility), death seems imminent. Should he pray for healing? Perhaps. And perhaps not. Sometimes, the best thing is to prepare everyone for what now looks like the will of God. And when we are ready to die, knowing what lies on the other side, it is better to look death in the face and say, "I do not fear you! Jesus has taken the sting of death away. He is the resurrection and the life, and though I die, yet shall I live." (cf. John 11:25).

THE FEAR OF DEATH

Paul told the Philippians of his own assurance of heaven. If he died, he would go into the presence of Jesus. Absent from the body, present with the Lord was how he understood it (Phil. 1:23). And because he knew it, he did not fear death.

But sometimes we do fear death and the devil plays on our weakness. He knows that we fear *dying*. Bildad, in an electrifying speech about death speaks of it as "the king of terrors" (Job 18:14). The author of Hebrews describes this fear as a form of "slavery" that the devil employs to his advantage (Heb. 2:15). When this fear grips, all talk of death becomes taboo. In part, it explains western culture and its almost complete avoidance of death. It is not uncommon, for example, for someone in their thirties or forties never to have seen a dead body. In almost total contrast to previous generations, most people today do not die in their homes. And when they are dead, their bodies are removed and beautified and rarely put on display as in previous generations.

But death *cannot* hurt Christians, not in the ultimate sense. Donald Grey Barnhouse, one-time Senior Minister of Tenth Presbyterian Church in Philadelphia, lost his wife when his daughter was still a child. In an attempt to help his daughter process the loss, he recounted an incident whilst driving along the highway. A large moving truck passed them casting a shadow over them as it drove by. Dr. Barnhouse asked his daughter, "Which would you prefer? To be run over by the truck or to have its shadow cast upon you?" His daughter replied immediately, "The shadow—because it can't hurt me." "And death is like that," replied Dr. Barnhouse, "it is like a shadow. But it cannot hurt you."[2]

It is said, with some justification, that eighteenth-century Methodists "died well." The observation comes in the wake of a period when Methodism, sprung from the roots of the Great Awakening[3], knew the gospel intimately and the assurance of salvation and eternal life which is its fruit. Dying well—in the sure and certain hope of everlasting life and immediate access to the near-presence of the reigning Lord Jesus Christ—became a Methodist trademark. Paul expresses the same confidence from his prison in Rome when he assured the Philippians that death would merely bring him closer to Jesus.

BLESSED ASSURANCE

Robert Bruce, the great Scottish minister, on the day of his death in 1631 ate an egg for breakfast. He enjoyed it so much that he asked his daughter Martha to prepare him another. Then, hesitating, he said, "No. There's no need. My master is calling me. Bring rather the Bible. Turn to the eighth chapter of Romans and put my finger on the words, 'I am persuaded that neither death, nor life ... shall

---

2   There are several versions of this story. One can be found in Timothy Keller, *Walking with God Through Pain and Suffering* (New York, NY: Dutton, 2013), p. 317.

3   The Great Awakening was a revival that occurred in Europe and North America in the 1730s and 1740s. Hundreds of thousands of people came to faith during these two decades through the preaching of men like Jonathan Edwards, George Whitefield, John Wesley and Samuel Davies.

be able to separate me from the love of God, which is in Jesus Christ my Lord."' Martha did this. "Is my finger on it?" he asked. Being assured it was he turned to her and said, "Now, God be with you my dear daughter: I have breakfasted with you, but I shall have supper with my Lord Jesus Christ this night." Soon Bruce was dead. And immediately passed into the presence of the Lord Jesus.

In the upper room, facing His own imminent death, Jesus reassured His anxious disciples. "Let not your hearts be troubled. Believe in God; believe also in me. In my Father's house are many rooms. If it were not so, would I have told you that I go to prepare a place for you? And if I go and prepare a place for you, I will come again and will take you to myself, that where I am you may be also. And you know the way to where I am going." (John. 14:1–4)

If only we knew when we were going to die! But the time of our death is uncertain—uncertain *to us*, that is. It is "appointed" by God (Heb. 9:27). It exists on a divine calendar of events. There is nothing random or contingent about it.

A JOURNEY

Death is not the end; it is the start of another journey. Paul uses the word "departure" (Phil. 1:23, *analysai*) to refer to death. He uses the same word later when writing what would be his final New Testament letter: "… the time of my *departure* has come" (2 Tim. 4:6). Death is like getting on a train, or bus or an airplane that will take us to heaven.

F. B. Meyer wrote a postcard to his friend as he was dying, "I have raced you to heaven, I am just off—see you there. Love F. B. Meyer."

How is such confidence possible?

There is the need for faith.

Faith in Jesus Christ and Him crucified.

Faith in Jesus Christ *alone* apart from any effort on our part to justify us before God.

Faith that receives what is offered in the gospel—forgiveness of sins and the spotless robe of Christ.

Faith in what Martin Luther called, *The Great Exchange*: our sins reckoned to Christ and His obedience reckoned to us.

Faith in Scripture, God's Word which as Jesus said, cannot be *broken* (John 10:35).

Faith in God's promises which are trustworthy and true. Grand promises like this one:

Who shall separate us from the love of Christ? Shall tribulation, or distress, or persecution, or famine, or nakedness, or danger, or sword? As it is written,

> *"For your sake we are being killed all the day long;*
> *we are regarded as sheep to be slaughtered."*

No, in all these things we are more than conquerors through him who loved us. For I am sure that neither death nor life, nor angels nor rulers, nor things present nor things to come, nor powers, nor height nor depth, nor anything else in all creation, will be able to separate us from the love of God in Christ Jesus our Lord. (Rom. 8:35–39)

Christians have every reason to believe that heaven awaits them when they die.

Chapter 3
Falling Asleep

... Truly, I say to you, today you will be with me in paradise.
—Jesus' final words to the dying thief (Luke 23:43)

Carved on the "Shannon" headstone (erected in 1857) in Balmoral Cemetery, Belfast, Northern Ireland are the following lines:

Stop traveller and cast an eye,
As you are now so once was I,
Prepare in time make no delay
For youth and time will pass away.

There are many variants of these lines, on many headstones. On a similar inscription on a tombstone in Indiana, an unknown author added two more lines:

> *To follow you I'm not content*
> *Until I know which way you went.*[1]

In the first chapter, we saw that in the parable of the rich man and Lazarus the Bible teaches a *conscious* existence after death. Lazarus died and was taken to "Abraham's side"—a euphemism for heaven. In the second chapter, we noted Paul's words to the Philippians in anticipation of the possibility that he might be executed. As he thought about his departure, he viewed it as something that would result in him being "with Christ" (Phil. 1:23), an existence which was "gain" and "far better" (1:21, 23).

Is it possible to know with certainty what will occur immediately after death?

Some describe "out-of-body" experiences where they "see" their bodies lying on a hospital bed as they float somehow upwards to the ceiling, all the while having some consciousness of viewing their bodies from this elevated position. In the long run, these experience-based descriptions fail to convince and recent retractions only further compromise these testimonies.

What can we expect when we die? What does the Bible say? Earlier, in the first chapter, we noted Jesus' words to the dying thief: "… Truly, I say to you, today you will

---

1   Randy Alcorn cites the Indiana version in *Heaven* (Carol Stream, IL: Tyndale, 2004), p. 33.

be with me in paradise" (Luke 23:43). Christians go to "paradise," which, as we saw in the first chapter, is another way of saying heaven.

A BUILDING, A HOUSE, AND CLOTHING

Writing to the Corinthians, Paul gives a somewhat extended account of what happens at death:

> *For we know that if the tent that is our earthly home is destroyed, we have a building from God, a house not made with hands, eternal in the heavens. For in this tent we groan, longing to put on our heavenly dwelling, if indeed by putting it on we may not be found naked. For while we are still in this tent, we groan, being burdened—not that we would be unclothed, but that we would be further clothed, so that what is mortal may be swallowed up by life. He who has prepared us for this very thing is God, who has given us the Spirit as a guarantee.*
>
> *So we are always of good courage. We know that while we are at home in the body we are away from the Lord, for we walk by faith, not by sight. Yes, we are of good courage, and we would rather be away from the body and at home with the Lord. So whether we are at home or away, we make it our aim to please him. For we must all appear before the judgment seat of Christ, so that each one may receive what is due for what he has done in the body, whether good or evil.* (2 Cor. 5:1–10)

We are jars of clay, fragile and easily broken. Paul is contemplating life and death in this current body of ours.

The treasure of the gospel that comforted him each day is stored in "jars of clay," jars that can break at any moment (2 Cor. 4:7). Life in this world is often harsh and difficult and therefore "death is at work in us," Paul concludes (2 Cor. 4:12). Our lives appear to be "wasting away" (2 Cor. 4:16), a figure of speech all too real for those who experience the ravages of old age and disease. Life can be unbearably harsh.

Life is a little bit like camping. Our lives are like a fragile tent that is easily blown down (2 Cor. 5:2, 4). My experience of sleeping in tents is a brief one. Apart from some luxury tents in France (they had electricity, fridges and a power supply), I have only spent one night in what most consider a tent. Erected by a friend and offered to me and my family for a week, we spent less than half a night in it. It was raining upon arrival and by early morning water was flowing through it. Having not slept we decided to go home and check the box, "slept in a tent" never to try it again.

Fragile and breakable, our "earthly tent" will eventually collapse. In the blinking of an eye, we pass from this world into the next. And then what? We experience *life,* is Paul's answer.

LIFE

Death "is swallowed up by *life,*" Paul writes (2 Cor. 5:4). After death, Christians are more alive than they have ever been. They are in the presence of Christ, *and they know it.*

But doesn't Scripture say that at death, we experience *sleep*? Several passages in Scripture employ this term:

- Describing a localized resurrection of the dead that occurred in Jerusalem after Jesus' resurrection, Matthew says, "… many bodies of the saints who had *fallen asleep* were raised" (Matt. 27:52).
- Jesus said of Jairus' deceased twelve-year-old daughter, "… she is not dead but *sleeping*" (Luke 8:52).
- Jesus spoke to His disciples about Lazarus, who had been dead for two days, "… Our friend Lazarus has *fallen asleep*, but I go to awaken him" (John 11:11).
- When Stephen was stoned to death, Luke writes, "… he fell asleep" (Acts 7:60).
- Recalling the witnesses to the resurrection of Christ, Paul mentions five hundred brothers who saw Him at once, adding "… some have *fallen asleep*" (1 Cor. 15:6).
- Paul urges the Thessalonians, "we do not want you to be uninformed, brothers, about those who are *asleep*, that you may not grieve as others do who have no hope" (1 Thess. 4:13).

From an observational point of view, death *is* like falling asleep. Some die violently and painfully but, even then, when the moment arrives, they close their eyes and appear to fall asleep.

Sleep is usually a very desirable experience; but not always. Jonathan Edwards, in a sermon on Acts 19:19, complained that some of his congregation slept during his preaching.[2] Difficult to imagine perhaps, that during the preaching of the greatest theologian America has ever produced, people fell asleep and lay down in the pews!

Sleep deprivation, for whatever reason, is debilitating. We need to sleep. It is a welcome release from the toil of the day. And dying is like falling asleep at the end of a long, hard day. We have no need to be afraid of it. On the contrary, it is a friend. Especially if we know where this will take us. Not to a land of dreams and unconsciousness, but to wake up on the other side in a place of glory and beauty and the presence of Jesus.

CLOTHING

A Presbyterian minister once told me, "You are what you wear!" It was a comment he made in response to an observation that someone had made in his presence that he was always "sartorially elegant." He was, without doubt, the smartest Presbyterian minister in the Presbytery. Clothes tell a story, as the fashion industry knows all too well.

In describing the transition from this world to the next, Paul employs the metaphor of clothing.

For in this tent we groan, longing to put on our heavenly dwelling, if indeed by putting it on we may not be found

---

2   Edwards complains further that people were "lying down" in the pews during the worship service! *The Blessing of God: Previously Unpublished Sermons of Jonathan Edwards*, ed. Michael D. McMullen, (Nashville, TN: Broadman & Holman, 2003), p. 270.

naked. For while we are still in this tent, we groan, being burdened—not that we would be unclothed, but that we would be further clothed, so that what is mortal may be swallowed up by life. (2 Cor. 5:2–4)

What does Paul mean when he says that after death, the believer may expect to be "further clothed"? Changing the metaphor, what does Paul mean when he introduces this section by saying that at death "… we have a building from God, a house not made with hands, eternal in the heavens" (2 Cor. 5:1)?

A building. Clothes. Since our bodies do not accompany us on this initial journey to heaven, what are we to make of these physical, tangible metaphors? Will our souls have some physicality to them in heaven, *before* the resurrection of our earthly bodies? This requires some explanation.

"We have a building …" The verb is in the present tense. Paul is not saying, "We will have a building," in the sense that at the resurrection, our bodies will rise from the grave to be reunited with our souls. That is true, but it is not what Paul is saying here. Paul is talking about the experience of heaven *immediately after death.*[3]

---

3   Some commentators think that the metaphors of a building and clothing refer to the future resurrection body, rather than the experience of the intermediate state. Paul has therefore "telescoped" the trajectory from death to future resurrection. This leads some to speculate that the experience of the intermediate state is itself "instantaneous" for the believer, passing through it "in an instant." These remain highly speculative notions. F. F. Bruce, for example, comments: "In

Some have concluded that Paul is referring to a *temporary physical body* of some kind.[4] At death, therefore, we enter a new existence which has physical dimensions. And, to some extent at least, this must be the case. After all, the physical body of Jesus is there! Truth is, we cannot begin to imagine what consciousness is devoid of a physical body. Even when we dream in a state of unconsciousness, we do so employing the physical brain. How can we speak and hear and see if we have no mouth, or ears, or eyes?

Most Bible scholars resist the idea of a temporary physical body at death, as do Reformed Confessions and Catechisms. Typical is the following question and answer of the *Westminster Shorter Catechism*:

Q. *What benefits do believers receive from Christ at death?*
A. The souls of believers are at their death made perfect in holiness, and do immediately pass into glory; and their

---

the consciousness of the departed believer there is no interval between dissolution and investiture, however long the interval may be by the calendar of earth-bound human history." F. F. Bruce, *Paul: The Apostle of the Heart Set Free* (Grand Rapids, MI: Eerdmans, 1977), p. 212–40.

4 Among others, Philip Edgcumbe Hughes and Herman Ridderbos have adopted a view of a temporary body after death. Philip E. Hughes, New International Commentary on the New Testament, *Paul's Second Epistle to the Corinthians* (Grand Rapids, MI: Eerdmans, 1962), pp. 160–161; Herman Ridderbos, *Paul*, trans. John Richard de Witt (Grand Rapids, MI: Eerdmans, 1975), pp. 499–501.

bodies, being still united to Christ, do rest in their graves till the resurrection.[5]

BODY AND SOUL

We are both body *and soul*. And at death, the soulish part of us exists in heaven. Though it is customary to hear some saying, "we *have* an immortal soul," it is better (and more biblical) to say, "we *are* a soul." In the description of creation in Genesis 1, for example, we read of "… every beast … every bird … everything that creeps on the earth … everything that has the *breath of life*" (Gen. 1:30). The word "breath" is rendered "living" in earlier verses in Genesis 1 (20, 21, 24, for example). In almost 300 later occurrences of the word ("*nephesh*" in Hebrew), it is translated "soul." My soul is the breath of life. It is consciousness. It is being self-aware. After death, we are *alive*.

On at least three occasions, the word "soul" is used in the New Testament to denote that aspect of a human being that continues *after* the death of our physical bodies:

And do not fear those who kill the body but cannot kill the soul. Rather fear him who can destroy both soul and body in hell. (Matt. 10:28)

… I saw under the altar the souls of those who had been slain for the word of God and for the witness they had borne. (Rev. 6:9)

---

5   Question and answer 37 of the *Westminster Shorter Catechism*.

... Also I saw the souls of those who had been beheaded for the testimony of Jesus and for the word of God ... (Rev. 20:4)

At death and beyond, we continue to live. In that sense, we are immortal. Our *soulishness* ensures our continued existence. According to this view, being "clothed upon" (or the metaphor of having a "building from God") is a way of saying that our experience of life after death will be greater and more certain than our current experience of it. We will experience life in a grander, more majestic way than ever before.

Said D. L. Moody: "Someday they'll tell you that Moody's dead. Don't believe it! That day I'll be before the throne; I'll be more alive than I've ever been." Death, for the believer, is an entrance into the sunshine of Jesus' immediate presence.

CERTAINTY

"We are always of good courage," Paul writes. He has a certainty about what happens when a believer dies:

... away from (ekdomeo) *the body ... at home* (endomeo) *with the Lord.* (2 Cor. 5:8)

It is one of the sweetest (and saddest) moments when we are permitted to see the passing of a believer from this world, and say, "they are in Jesus' presence now." We imagine them alive, thinking, seeing, hearing, laughing, dancing, singing, worshipping. Reunited with Christian friends and relatives, some of whom lived hundreds of years before them. Abraham, Elijah, Paul, Augustine, Luther … and *Jesus*. When this is our hope, we cannot grieve as those "… who have no hope" (1 Thess. 4:13). Our friends are in a better place and they would not—*do not*—wish to return. All we can do is ask for patience to wait and grace to persevere until we join them.

Christians are certain about heaven. And they are certain about how to get there.

Can we be *that* certain of heaven? When asked, "Are you going to heaven when you die?" what is *your* answer?

"I hope so!"

"That depends on how *good* I have been."

A hope that is built upon our own efforts to get into heaven will shatter into an infinite number of fragments. What "good" could the thief on the cross do before his death? And yet, he was assured of "paradise."

How can we be sure of heaven when we die?

The answer is *faith*. Faith *alone* in Jesus Christ *alone*, apart from any effort on our part.

> *Dear dying lamb, Thy precious blood*
> *Will never lose its power,*
> *Till all the ransomed church of God*
> *Be saved to sin no more.*
>
> *The dying thief rejoiced to see*
> *That fountain in his day,*

And there have I as blind as he
Washed all my sins away.[6]

COURAGE

Knowing what happens to us when we die makes us bold. "So we are always of good courage ... Yes, we are always of good courage ..." (2 Cor. 5:6, 8). In some translations, the word he uses for "courage" is rendered "confidence" two chapters later.[7]

Certainty encourages boldness.[8] Boldness *here* and *now*, that is. Courage to speak and do great things. Courage to be bold, regardless of the consequences. For what is the worst that can happen? We may die. And death, for the Christian, is the entry into heaven. What have we to fear?

Christians die with courage because they die with confidence. Think of Stephen facing death by stoning. With blood-stained eyes, he gazed into heaven and said, "... Behold, I see the heavens opened, and the Son of Man standing at the right hand of God" (Acts 7:56).

Stephen saw a glimpse of heaven before he died. He was certain of where he was going. And it made him bold.

Stephen was granted a glimpse of another part of the space-time universe where Jesus' body exists. The three dimensions of space that currently confine us, do so no longer in the case of the body of Jesus. His body ascended

---

6   These verses are contained in the hymn, "There is a Fountain Filled with Blood" by William Cowper (1731–1800).

7   "...I have complete confidence in you" (2 Cor. 7:16; cf. Heb. 13:6).

8   In the ESV, the word "confidence" used in 2 Corinthians 5:6 and 5:8 is rendered "boldness" in 2 Corinthians 10:2.

into a cloud (Acts 1:9). His body passed through what we might call a "fold" in space, into another realm of the created universe. And Stephen caught a glimpse of this realm. And soon thereafter, he entered it himself.

Knowing the journey ahead with certainty enables us to face it with courage. Christians are going to meet Jesus when they die.

Chapter 4
The Trumpet Shall Sound

… we believe that Jesus … through Jesus, God will bring with him those who have fallen asleep. (1 Thess. 4:14)

A venerable opinion exists, stemming largely from the philosophical traditions of Aristotle and Plato, that knowledge is a virtue. Our mind matters. We are meant to explore and discover new boundaries of knowledge. We are meant to know and understand certain things.

The Second Coming and the constellation of events that accompany it, including the resurrection of those who have "fallen asleep," are truths that Christians are meant to know. "… [W]e do not want you to be uninformed …"

Paul told the Thessalonian Christians (1 Thess. 4:13), about certain truths, some of which had been circulating for a while, and some Paul said came to him "… by a word from the Lord …" (1 Thess. 4:15).

One such truth concerns the faithful dead, currently with Jesus: are they going to miss the greatest spectacle on earth—the Second Coming?

To be honest, this may not sound like a particularly important issue. And the reason lies with the degree to which the Second Coming figures in our thinking. For the early Christians, talk about the Second Coming had a greater sense of anticipation than it seems to have for many Christians today. For all they knew, the interval between the ascension and the Second Coming might only be a generation or two. In which case, they might still be alive when it happened. And if they were to be alive, some interesting questions arise: will the departed in heaven, currently dis-embodied, receive a resurrection body? Will those who are alive at Jesus' Second Coming be reunited with their departed friends and relatives? And, do we have any real estimate as to *when* the Second Coming might occur?

Near, Far, at Any Moment?

Interestingly, as Paul writes to the Thessalonian Christians, he includes himself among those who may be alive when Jesus returns: "… we who are alive, who are left until the coming of the Lord …" (1 Thess. 4:15). In later epistles (Philippians, for example), Paul demonstrates an expectation that he may die before Jesus returns (Phil. 1:20).

Did Paul change his mind? Some have made much of this possibility, suggesting that Paul's theology, on this issue and many other matters, evolved and changed. There is an "early Paul" and a "late Paul" and the New Testament can't be trusted. The trajectory of insinuation is designed to undermine certainty and confidence. It has been the stuff of debate for over a century. It is a narrative of skepticism about Scripture's trustworthiness.

Whether Paul initially believed that Jesus would return within his lifetime or not seems innocent enough. He was not privy to the date of the Lord's return and it is perfectly understandable that he believed in the possibility that Jesus might return within his lifetime. Revising his view of the possibility of death is very different from the allegations that Paul revised his entire thinking about the Second Coming and matters relating to it.

Early Christians do appear to have believed that the "End" was near-at-hand. For example, when Jesus predicted the destruction of the temple (an event that took place during the sacking of Jerusalem in A.D. 70), the disciples seemed to think that such an event would indeed usher in the "… end of the age" (Matt. 24:3).

Soon or Right Now?

Believing that Jesus is going to return "soon" and believing that it can happen "at any moment" are two very different ideas. Does the New Testament teach that Jesus can return in the next five seconds?

The question is important. If, for example, the New Testament teaches that an event (or a series of events) must occur *before* Jesus returns, then clearly, Jesus *cannot* be said to return *at any moment*. What events might these be? Some examples would be the preaching of the gospel in all the world (Matt. 24:14), and the appearance of the "man of sin" (2 Thess. 2:3–10). We need not explore what either of these mean just now. That such markers exist at all indicates that Jesus' return cannot be in the next five seconds. If these passages predict an event that has not yet occurred (and this is an important caveat) *and* that the event must occur *before* Jesus' return, then the "any moment" view of Jesus' Second Coming is misguided.

The "any moment" view of the Second Coming was bolstered by the belief that the Second Coming involves a two-fold "coming" of Christ at the end of age. The first aspect of this coming may occur at any moment, without warning; the second aspect after a more predictable trajectory.

In 1 Thessalonians 4:17, for example, Paul speaks of believers being "caught up" to meet the Lord in the air. In the Latin Vulgate translation, the verb is rendered "*rapiemur*", or in English, "raptured." According to this view, Jesus is thought to come *for* the saints "at any moment." Resurrected saints and saints who are still alive will be "raptured" to the clouds to meet Jesus and thereafter be taken to the seven-year marriage feast of the Lamb.[1] During this period, all kinds of events occur including a period of tribulation, culminating in the Great Tribulation. Armies of the beast and the false prophet will gather to do battle against the people of God. Once this feast is over, Jesus will then return *with* the saints and this time descend all the way down to the earth and take His throne in Jerusalem.

Note the following:

- Jesus comes in two stages: *for* the saints and *with* the saints.[2]
- Stage one will include a rapture and only in the second stage of His coming will Jesus descend to the earth.
- The rapture stage is "at any moment" whereas the second stage will be seven years later.

If Jesus is not expected to return "at any moment," should we also dismiss the idea that Jesus will return "soon"? No. This would be unsafe and presumptive. All the events that must occur before Jesus returns could occur in a relatively short period, certainly within a generation. The wisest policy therefore is to live with the *possibility* (that's different from saying *probability*) that Jesus might return before we die. *If* that were to occur, we would not ourselves experience the intermediate state. Our bodies would

---

1   The seven-year marriage supper of the Lamb is a view derived from a synthesis of the seventieth week of Daniel 9 and Revelation 19:7-9.

2   Note that the coming of Jesus "with" the saints occurs in 1 Thess. 3:13 and 4:14.

therefore experience a transformation that befits our new residence—a transformed earth.

Secret Coming?

The belief that Jesus can return "at any moment", and that we might not know it (unbelievers, for example, would experience the phenomenon that people have "disappeared"), is sometimes referred to as the "*secret rapture*". According to this view the Second Coming (at least its initial phase) is a secret event. But the New Testament describes the Second Coming as a *noisy* event! Far from being a *secret*, the Second Coming involves the sound of a trumpet.

Trumpets are noisy. In a one-hundred-piece orchestra, with all the instruments playing loudly, the trumpets will always overpower the rest. Conductors, especially of less disciplined orchestras, can often be seen gesturing the brass to lay up a little. I once attended a rehearsal of a major symphony orchestra when the conductor said some rather unpleasant things to the brass section because they were playing too loudly. In their embarrassment, they asked me to leave.

Trumpets sounded at Sinai saying in effect, "the LORD is here" (Exod. 19:13, 16, 19; 20:18).

Trumpets foretold Pentecost, saying in effect, "the LORD is here" (Joel 2:1, 15).

Trumpets accompany the Second Coming, saying in effect, "the LORD is here" (1 Thess. 4:16).

There is nothing secret about the Second Coming! When it happens, everyone will know it.

And at the Second Coming, a magnificent transformation will take place. The order of things will change. And there will be no advantage at all in being alive when Jesus comes. The first thing Jesus will do is raise the dead. Bodies will rise from the grave ... "the dead in Christ will rise first" (1 Thess. 4:16).

Paul describes it using two quite different ideas. The dead will come *with* Jesus, and the dead will rise to *meet* Jesus:

> ... *at the coming of our Lord Jesus with all his saints.* (1 Thess. 3:13)

> ... *God will bring with [Jesus] those who have fallen asleep.* (1 Thess. 4:14)

> ... *we who are alive, who are left, will be caught up together with them in the clouds to meet the Lord in the air.* (1 Thess. 4:17)

How can those who come "*with* Jesus" rise and "*meet*" Him "in the air"? The answer is simple. When the saints die, they leave half of themselves behind! What is in view here is the reunion of the soul and resurrected body.

What a marvelous thing it would be not to experience death—the separation of body and soul! It is an unnatural thing. Had Adam and Eve not sinned, there would have been no experience of human death. But Paul's point is to say that even if we die, this will be of no disadvantage when it comes to the Second Coming. We will rise and meet the Lord in the air and be reunited with the other half of ourselves, our souls. And we, who have always been alive in a soulish way, will be alive *in our bodies* again. The morning of resurrection has arrived.

Right now, these bodies of ours grow frail and decay. They wear out. Bits and pieces no longer work. Some parts have been replaced. And for some, every day in this body is a struggle. Disease has made life in this body a daily torture. In our present status, we "… groan inwardly as we wait eagerly for adoption as sons, the redemption of our bodies" (Rom. 8:23). Soon, we will "sleep", our bodies will be laid to rest to await the resurrection morning.

But all that is going to change.

Death is going to be transformed. Jesus told Jairus that his daughter who had died was sleeping. People laughed. But He raised her from the dead and stopped their laughing (Mark 5:41–42). He will do the same on resurrection morning.

Grief is going to be transformed—in our future existence, there will be no more tears.

> He will wipe away every tear from their eyes, and death shall be no more, neither shall there be mourning, nor crying, nor pain anymore, for the former things have passed away. (Rev. 21:4)

Hope will be transformed. Thessalonian Christians were grieving the loss of loved ones. And Paul's aim was to help them see beyond the temporary loss, and a vision of a beautiful future of transformation and reunion. Do not grieve as though there is no hope, Paul says to them, because there is hope, marvelous and certain hope involving resurrection and fullness of life (1 Thess. 4:13).

"The dead have no hope." That was the world Paul lived in. It is the world we also live in. Great Britain's most eminent scientist, Stephen Hawking, pronounced in an exclusive interview in *The Guardian* newspaper that belief in a heaven or an afterlife is "a fairy story."[3] But for Paul, who had witnessed Jesus' own resurrection, nothing could be more certain for a believer than the belief that when we die, our souls are with Jesus in a conscious state and, when Jesus returns, our souls will be clothed with the physicality of a resurrected body.

THE PERSONAL TOUCH

Jesus is returning personally. As we have seen, there is no advantage to being alive when this happens; the dead will be advantaged and have a place of priority in the proceedings—a front row seat, as it were. "For the Lord *himself*[4] will descend from heaven ..." (1 Thess. 4:16).

Luke tells us something very similar: "... This Jesus, who was taken up from you into heaven, will come in the same way as you saw him go into heaven" (Acts 1:11).

---

3   https://www.theguardian.com/science/2011/may/15/stephen-hawking-interview-there-is-no-heaven. Accessed 06/03/17.

4   The word "himself" is not in the Greek text, but it is the intent of the verse.

The entire event has drama written all over it. We have already noted the drama associated with trumpet blasts announcing that the Lord is coming. Trumpets get your attention. In addition, there are two more features that we should notice:

- The cry of command (1 Thess. 4:16). Who will give it? The Father? He alone knows when this event is to take place (cf. Matt. 24:36).
- The accompaniment of an archangel (1 Thess. 4:16). Only one archangel is mentioned in the Bible—Michael (Jude 9).[5] In the opening verse of Daniel 10, Michael is described as a great heavenly power who stands in defense of Messiah and his people (Dan. 10:13, 21). In Revelation, he leads the cosmic forces of heaven in war against the dragon (Satan) and his armies (Rev. 12:7).

Trumpets, a cry of command, an archangel and *Jesus* in His resplendent glory! All this takes place "up there" in the clouds, in the air. Symbolism abounds here, of course. Clouds remind us of the presence of God—the "cloudy pillar" at the time of the Exodus; the clouds at Jesus' transfiguration (Exod. 19:16; Matt. 17:5). The "air" is Satan's current domain in Scripture. He is "… the prince and power of the air" (Eph. 2:2). But he is going to be knocked off his pretentious perch. Jesus will reign supreme over the totality of creation.

---

5   Gabriel is sometimes said to be an archangel, but he is identified in Scripture as an "angel" (Luke 1:19, 26; cf. Dan. 8:16; 9:21).

And what follows the Second Coming is forever: Christians will be with the Lord "always" (1 Thess. 4:17).

Little wonder, then, that Paul says, "... encourage one another ..." as he concludes his study of the Second Coming (1 Thess. 4:18).

Christians look ahead and have a million reasons to be encouraged.

Chapter 5
The New Heaven and New Earth

*Then I saw a new heaven and a new earth, for the first
heaven and the first earth had passed away, and the sea
was no more.* (Rev. 21:1)

Some people go to surprising depths to make Christianity
look ridiculous. Speaking on BBC Radio during the Second
World War, C. S. Lewis addressed the skeptical reactions
people demonstrate to the idea of heaven as described in
the Bible:

> *There is no need to be worried by facetious people who
> try to make the Christian hope of "Heaven" ridiculous by
> saying they do not want "to spend eternity playing harps."
> The answer to such people is that if they cannot understand*

books written for grown-ups, they should not talk about them. All the scriptural imagery (harps, crowns, gold, etc.) is, of course, a merely symbolical attempt to express the inexpressible... People who take these symbols literally might as well think that when Christ told us to be like doves, He meant that we were to lay eggs.[1]

When the Bible talks about heaven, especially in its final form, it employs imagery and we need to appreciate its subtleties lest we make fools of ourselves.

So, let's ask the following question: where will believers spend eternity?

We are not thinking now about "heaven"—the location of believers in the intermediate state. We are thinking instead of the final location, after the Second Coming— the place referred to as "the new heaven and new earth" (Isa. 65:17; 66:22; 2 Pet. 3:13[2]; Rev. 21:1). It is one of the very last things the Bible talks about in the book of Revelation.

APOCALYPSE AND AFTER

The Book of Revelation takes us on a journey from the first century to the final state of the new heaven and earth. It tells the story of redemption using apocalyptic images taken from the Old Testament showing us the "story behind the story". On the surface is the Roman Empire

---

1   C. S. Lewis, *Mere Christianity* (Basingstoke, UK: MacMillan Publishers, 1977), p. 120.

2   The references in Isaiah and 2 Peter to "heaven" are in the plural "new heavens."

demonically at war against Christ and His people. But a larger narrative is being played out, one that first shows up in Genesis 3. It is the story of a slithering, talking serpent at war with God and His creation who grows into a great red dragon in the final book of Scripture (Rev. 12:3). The talking serpent-dragon is none other than Satan, God's most powerful enemy who is engaged in all-out war with "the seed of the woman"—God's elect children and ultimately God's own Son.

In the closing chapters of Revelation, John describes the destruction of Satan and his cohorts—the beast and the false prophet (depicting religious and secular powers in their combined resistance to Jesus and the gospel). And along with these characters, God also destroys what they have built—Babylon, the city of man implacably hostile to God, a monument to self-aggrandizement and pride. Set against Babylon is God's city, the New Jerusalem, the final dwelling place of God's people. And, since God also dwells in this city, the New Jerusalem is also a temple. God is preparing for His people a temple-city to live in forever.

An important observation is needed before we go any further. The final expectation in Scripture concerning what lies ahead is "… a new heaven and a new earth …" (Rev. 21:1). Specifically, we are to expect a new *earth*!

Earth! It is intended as something solid and physical rather than something spiritual and ethereal. Earth is comprised of rocks and hills, oceans and rivers, forests and fields, birds and animals. And human beings. And the *new* earth will comprise of these, too. Earth without the effects of the curse. Earth as it would have been had our first parents not sinned. No less physical and material than the one we now know.

"In its final form, what is heaven like?"

Answer: "Like this! But renewed and more glorious."

Creation Reborn

Think about what Paul writes in Romans 8:19–22:

> *For the creation waits with eager longing for the revealing of the sons of God. For the creation was subjected to futility, not willingly, but because of him who subjected it, in hope that the creation itself will be set free from its bondage to corruption and obtain the freedom of the glory of the children of God. For we know that the whole creation has been groaning together in the pains of childbirth until now.*

Creation, the physical universe and its contents, is waiting to be re-born. The stresses and strains it currently exhibits are birth pains. Redeemed human beings are going to exist in a world like this one, if we can imagine what it would be like had no sin ever entered it. Adam was created to live in and explore this world. He was given a mandate to subdue the earth and its livestock (Gen. 1:26–28). And, he was meant to go beyond the garden and bring the rest of the earth (and the cosmos) into a recognizable order and shape.

God could have made the entire universe a garden and spared Adam the bother of exploration and investigation, but He did not. God desires His most-treasured creation that bears His image to enjoy the task of survey, discovery, design and artistry. Made from the dust of the earth, humanity is the link, the *vicegerent*, between the earth and God. In subjugating it, humanity is meant to discover its maker and respond in worship and praise. This was the intent. Instead, Adam fell. Humankind turned in upon itself and worshipped the creature rather than the creator (Rom. 1:25). And though much has been discovered and subjugated, the credit has been given elsewhere instead of to God.

But change is coming. God is going to renew the world. Which world? *This one*—about which we already have some knowledge and experience. Yes, this world rather than a *brand new* world. And in this renewed cosmos, humanity will explore again, and give God all the glory.

Because of something Peter writes, some have drawn the conclusion that everything about this world, including matter itself, is going to be destroyed (annihilated) and a completely new universe brought into being. Peter writes, "… the heavens will pass away with a roar, and the heavenly bodies will be burned up and dissolved …" (2 Pet. 3:10).

The terms "burned up and dissolved" suggest a complete annihilation of this universe. Several considerations suggest that this explanation is incorrect:

- The Greek term for "new" ("a *new* heaven and a *new* earth") is "*kainos*" rather than "*neos*", suggesting new in quality rather than new in origin.

- Paul's metaphor in Romans 8 is one of *liberation* rather than destruction: "... the creation itself will be set free from its bondage to corruption ..." (Rom. 8:21).[3]
- There is both continuity and discontinuity between what we are now and what we will be in heaven. Jesus rose in the *same* body as the one that earlier was declared dead. Likewise, our resurrected bodies will share a continuity with our present bodies.
- The triumph of Jesus over Satan must surely be in such a way that does not grant him victory. An annihilation of the physical universe might imply that Satan has, in part, triumphed after all.[4]

One scholar puts it this way:

The world into which we shall enter in the Parousia of Jesus Christ is therefore not another world; it is this world, this heaven, this earth; both, however, passed away and renewed. It is these forests, these fields, these cities, these streets, these people, that will be the scene of redemption. At present they are battlefields, full of the strife and sorrow of the not-yet-accomplished consummation; then they will be fields of victory, fields of harvest, where out of seed that was sown with tears the everlasting sheaves will be reaped and brought home.[5]

---

3   It is the same verb employed in John 8:32, "the truth will set you free" (ἐλευθερόω).

4   For more on these issues, see, A. A. Hoekema, *The Bible and the Future* (Exeter, UK: Paternoster Press, 1978), pp. 280-281.

5   Emil Brunner, *Eternal Hope*, trans. Harold Knight (London, UK: Butterworth, 1954), p. 204.

The universe is going to be reborn; but, it is going to be this universe rather than some other one. And many of its features will be immediately recognizable.

THE CITY OF GOD

Writing in the fifth century, Augustine responded to the sustained allegation of secular thought that Christianity was inimical to civilization and government. The book, called *The City of God*, has a surprisingly contemporary feel to it. We, too, live in a culture that is increasingly hostile to faith in the civic realm. The mantra, "Believers need not apply", is heard loud and clear in our time. Reclaiming Babylon and turning it into something that looks more like Jerusalem often looks an impossible task. Try, we must. It is the mandate God has given to us. And one day, the other side of the Second Coming, the city will be reborn.

Babylon is heading for destruction: "… Fallen, fallen is Babylon the great! …" (Rev. 18:2). The city, currently ruled by the dragon, will give way to the New Jerusalem, a city created by God for the people of God to dwell in.

In apocalyptic terms, John describes a vast city of enormous proportions and security. And what he describes is in one sense fantastical and bizarre. A cube each side of which measures 1,400 miles (Rev. 21:15–17)! And walls that are 200 feet thick. What this signifies is a city that is as vast as it is safe.

And there is exquisite beauty, "… like a most rare jewel, like a jasper, clear as crystal" (Rev. 21:11). The walls and foundation stones are made of precious stones, jasper, sapphire, agate, emerald, onyx, carnelian, chrysolite, beryl, topaz, chrysoprase, jacinth and amethyst (Rev. 21:19–20). Each city gate is made of a single, gigantic pearl. And the streets are comprised of "... pure gold like transparent glass" (Rev. 21:21).

Glory! The city shines with "the glory of God" (Rev. 21:11; cf. 21:22–23; 22:5). It exudes God's majesty and significance. And since the Greek and Hebrew word for "glory" hints at "heaviness", the New Jerusalem is full of the weightiness of God's presence. God is everywhere in this city and His presence can be felt. In every conceivable way, this is the City of *God*! And one day, it will appear.

THE TEMPLE OF GOD

Metaphors change and now the New Jerusalem is a temple.[6] "And I saw no temple in the city, for its temple is the Lord God the Almighty and the Lamb" (Rev. 21:22). Temple is a way of describing God's presence. Throughout most of the Old Testament, God dwelt in a tabernacle-temple. In fact, the idea starts in Eden, a garden which functions as a temple, because God is there, walking about in the "... cool of the day ..." (Gen. 3:8). Eden is a garden-sanctuary where God dwells with His people.

---

6 For a full analysis of the image of temple in Scripture, see G. K. Beale, *The Temple and the Mission of God: A Biblical Theology of the Dwelling Place of God*, New Studies in Biblical Theology (Downers Grove, IL: IVP Academic, 2004), and the more recent, Greg Beale and Mitchell Kim, *God Dwells Among Us: Expanding Eden to the Ends of the Earth* (Downers Grove, IL: InterVarsity, 2014).

And the Bible ends in an Eden-like garden with access to the Tree of Life:

Then the angel showed me the river of the water of life, bright as crystal, flowing from the throne of God and of the Lamb through the middle of the street of the city; also, on either side of the river, the tree of life with its twelve kinds of fruit, yielding its fruit each month. The leaves of the tree were for the healing of the nations. (Rev. 22:1–2)

Scripture comes full circle. Instead of the wilderness, the earth becomes a garden.

In Eden, God commissions Adam and Eve to find fulfilment in worshipping Him. God's purpose is to make His presence known in all the earth. Humanity's priestly task in Eden—a task that culminates in spectacular failure—is to keep guard over the garden by obeying God's Word. The mandate to explore and subdue the earth is a command to turn the earth into a garden-sanctuary. The failure of Adam and Eve sets up the story of the Old Testament with its central feature of the tabernacle, reminiscent of an architect's scale-model of God's presence with His people and provision for their sin.

Christmas is also a temple story. In Jesus, God's temple is personified. Jesus *is* the temple. The child born in the manger is "Immanuel" meaning "God with us" (Matt. 1:23; cf. Isa. 7:14; 8:8). It is echoed in Revelation 21:

And I heard a loud voice from the throne saying, "Behold, the dwelling place of God is with man. He will dwell with

*them, and they will be his people, and God himself will be
with them as their God." (Rev. 21:3)*

Curiously, John saw no temple in the city; at least, no
physical temple: "And I saw no temple in the city, for its
temple is the Lord God the Almighty and the Lamb"
(Rev. 21:22). That's because Jesus in fellowship with His
redeemed people comprise the temple.

BRAVE NEW WORLD

What John describes using colored pictures is a place of
purity and perfection.

No longer will there be anything accursed ... (Rev. 22:3)

Because Jesus was made a curse for us (cf. Gal. 3:13), there
is nothing left of the curse in the new city-temple.

It is difficult to imagine a world without sin. But despite
this difficulty, we do long for it. We have an instinct that
desires something other than the here and now. "... I do
not do *what I want* ..." Paul says (Rom. 7:15). There is
always this "wanting," a sense that what there is now is not
what ought to be, or even will be.

I know what I want—to be free from sin's down-drag
on my life and the life of others.

I know what I want—to live in a place where there's joy
and happiness and fulfilment.

I know what I want—to be who I was intended to be.

When sin is no more, sin's pain will also be no more.
Pain is a consequence of the curse. Not all pain is bad.

Some is positively beneficial. Without a central nervous system, we would not know that fire can burn our flesh. It is a good instinct to pull our hand away. Whether we will experience this kind of pain in the new heaven and earth is unclear. Perhaps we will, and our bodies will feel the sense of touch, the sharpness of an edge, the heat of a fire, the comfort of a chair, the softness of a bed.

But there will be no cruel pain, no pain that causes regret and loss. Those tears are wiped away (Rev. 21:4). God, who puts our tears in a bottle (Ps. 56:8), reassures us of His tender comfort and says, there will be no tears of pain, this kind of pain, in the world to come. None!

Heaven, the final state of it, is a *safe* place. There are no dangers left on the outside to threaten those who occupy this garden-city-temple. The gates of the city are open (Rev. 21:25). There is no fear of attack. Danger is eradicated. The dragon will be locked in the bottomless pit never to threaten again.

Safety is what is meant by the otherwise enigmatic statement: "… and the sea was no more" (Rev. 21:1). We are not meant to conclude that there will be no oceans and therefore no sailing, or water-sports, or marine life, or fishing, or snorkeling. Some, lacking the sensitivity required in interpreting apocalyptic genre, have suggested that the new heaven and new earth will lack all forms of water. Others have suggested that there will be an absence of salt-water but not of natural, fresh water. This is to miss the symbolism intended. The sea in biblical times was a hostile place. Despite having access to the Mediterranean, the Jews were not a sea-faring people. Thus, in Daniel's visions, monsters rise from the sea (Dan. 7: 1–8), something which is echoed in Revelation when a beast of the sea appears (Rev. 13:1). The sea is where Leviathan, the sea-monster, resides (Job 3:8; 41:1; Ps. 104:26). No such ogres will occupy the seas of the new earth.

And who will be found in new earth? The "nations," the redeemed from every tribe and people and tongue (Rev. 21:24, 26). The mandate of the Great Commission, reflecting the promise given to Abraham at the very beginning, was to make disciples of "all nations" (Matt. 28:19; cf. Gen. 12:2). On the Mount of Olives, Jesus carefully explained to the disciples that the Second Coming could not occur until the gospel is preached in all the nations (Matt. 24:14). And in the end, they will come to the city-garden-temple of the new heaven and new earth from every tribe and people-group. They will enter the city's gates and worship the Lord there. And presumably, their ethnic identity will remain apparent as a sign of God's multifaceted grace put on display.

It's all about Worship

And Jesus will be there. The pinnacle of what John sees is in the description given of the worship offered in the new temple: "… the throne of God and of the Lamb will be in it, and his servants will worship him" (Rev. 22:3).

Does the thought of worship sound dull and unexciting to you? Who wants to spend eternity worshipping God? God's redeemed children do. It is instinctive. They want to worship Him all the time. In formal settings with others and in private settings when engaged in their favorite pastime.

Having experienced the grace of the gospel, worship is a reflex. All of life is an act of worship, now as much as it will be then. Doxology is what we were made for. If we have no desire for it here and now, we will inevitably find descriptions of an eternity of worship disturbing.

At the heart of worship is the Son. In the New Jerusalem, the new city-garden-temple, there will be no night (Rev. 22:5). It is an odd statement, not intended as a scientific, astronomical indication that there will be no sun, or moon, or planetary systems, or stars in the renewed cosmos. Eventually, our present sun will burn itself out. And though I have no scientific explanation for the concept of eternal light issuing from a sun, for my part, I fully expect a universe full of stars and galaxies— the same ones we now see. And it thrills me no end to think that travel to one of them may be possible.

What John means is that here and now we see in a glass darkly (1 Cor. 13:12), but there we will see Him face to face. He will be the light that compares to no other light. He will outshine the sun. As Anne Cousin put it:

The bride eyes not her garment, but her dear bridegroom's face
I will not gaze at glory, but on my King of grace;
Not at the crown he gifteth, but on his pierced hand:
The Lamb is all the glory of Emmanuel's land.[7]

The greatest part of the new heaven and new earth is seeing Jesus in all His glory.

---

7   From the hymn, 'The sands of time are sinking', first published in the 1860s. It was inspired by the last words of Samuel Rutherford (1600-1661).

Chapter 6
What Will Heaven be Like?

And God saw everything that he had made, and behold, it was very good. (Gen. 1:31)

For we know that the whole creation has been groaning together in the pains of childbirth until now. (Rom. 8:22)

But the day of the Lord will come like a thief, and then the heavens will pass away with a roar, and the heavenly bodies will be burned up and dissolved, and the earth and the works that are done on it will be exposed. (2 Pet. 3:10)

What will heaven *in its final form* be like?

We have already answered this question in part using the imagery of Revelation 21 and 22. Heaven in its final state will be like a new city, a new temple, a new garden and a new world.

A new world? How new?

Will we recognize it?

What will we do there?

What will *we* be like?

Will we be able to walk, and run and swim? Will we eat food? Will we work *and* play? And sleep? And play golf? Even if we never played it here?

Questions now multiply like flies on a summer day. Come to think of it, will there be *flies* and *seasons* in the new heaven and earth?

But we run ahead of ourselves. First we need to be clear about what heaven itself will be like.

We have already dismissed thoughts of puffy clouds and winged, cherub-like infants floating around, playing harps or the like. Hymns are not always helpful at this point. Too many of them suggest lines like,

> *Where the harps of angels ring,*
> *And the blest forever sing.*[1]

And some even suggest that there will be no work to be done:

> *Be not aweary, for labor will cease some glad morning;*
> *Turmoil will change to infinite peace, some glad morning.*[2]

We need to think more concretely. Cities, lakes, rivers, buildings, trees, flowers, and animals and birds and fish! We need to imagine a universe to be discovered and explored. Suddenly thoughts of heaven change dramatically.

So, let's go back to the beginning. After all, last things are about first things as they should have been and would

---

1   William J. Kirkpatrick, "Meet Me There" (1838–1921).

2   Charlotte Homer, "Some Bright Morning" (1856–1932).

have been had Adam and Eve not sinned. Last things are about a "new heaven and new earth," just like first things: "In the beginning, God created the heavens and the earth" (Gen. 1:1).

A NEW EARTH

C. S. Lewis's *The Last Battle* captures something of the sense that the new earth will be strangely familiar to us, as though we had been here before. As Lucy and her friends pass through the threshold of Aslan's country (heaven) mourning the loss of *Narnia*, they find themselves overcome by a sense that the terrain is strangely familiar. Edmund (Lucy's brother) points out familiar mountain ranges. Farsight (the eagle) then soars on high and descends to say, "We have all been blind. We are only beginning to see...this is Narnia." And as they talk among themselves as to how this could be, one of their number explains:

When Aslan said you could never go back to Narnia, he meant the Narnia you were thinking of. But that was not the real Narnia. That had a beginning and an end. It was only a shadow or a copy of the real Narnia which has always been here and always will be here: just as our world, England and all, is only a shadow or copy of something in Aslan's real world.

You may have been in a room in which there was a window that looked out on a lovely bay of the sea or a green valley that wound away among mountains. And in the wall of that room opposite to the window there may have been a looking-glass. And as you turned away from the window you suddenly caught sight of that sea or that valley, all over again, in the looking glass. And the sea in the mirror, or the valley in the mirror, were in one sense just the same as the real ones: yet at the same time they were somehow different—deeper, more wonderful, more like places in a story: in a story you have never heard but very much want to know. The difference between the old Narnia and the new Narnia was like that. The new one was a deeper country: every rock and flower and blade of grass looked as if it meant more. I can't describe it any better than that: if ever you get there you will know what I mean.[3]

A deeper country, more real and glorious than the one we already know.

There are important principles involved in thinking about the final state of things this way. Christianity affirms the material order. God creates a physical world and human beings comprised of flesh and blood. We should not be surprised, therefore, that the new order will also be a material order with redeemed human beings comprised of flesh and blood. Few truths are more central to Christianity than the physical incarnation and resurrection of the body of Christ. In the consummation, we will once again inhabit physical bodies, localized in space and time, in an environment suited to our physicality.

---

3   C. S. Lewis, *The Last Battle* (New York, NY: Collier Books, 1956), pp. 168–171.

There is every reason to believe that we will experience the new order spatially *and* temporally. It is a mistranslation to render Revelation 10:6 as "there shall be time no longer" (KJV). The ESV correctly translates the word "time" as "delay" suggesting something quite different. This verse led some, including the venerable Abraham Kuyper, to suggest that there is "no time" in heaven.[4] But this seems misguided. If there is space (and a finite, corporeal resurrection body suggest space and a zip code), there will most certainly be time. We may experience both space and time differently, but we shall always be found in an environment of locality and sequence. The very idea of travel, or discovery, or learning requires a "before" and an "after."

DOGS IN HEAVEN

To make this issue of continuity between the world we know and the world to come, let's ask the simple question, "Are there dogs in heaven?" I put it this way because I like dogs. It is hard to imagine life without them. My instinct is to respond to inquiries about dogs in heaven by saying, "Of course, there are!"

True, dogs are said to be "outside" the New Jerusalem in the final chapter of Scripture (Rev. 22:15). But this is imagery. And the image is of wild, savage dogs rather than

---

4   Abraham Kuyper, *The Revelation of St. John* (Eugene, OR: Wipf and Stock Publications, 1999), ad. loc. In similar fashion, the hymn, "When the roll is called up yonder," includes the line, "And time shall be no more." The hymn was written by James Milton Black in 1893.

Jake, or Luther, or Gracie (names of dogs I have loved). Nothing that savages will occupy the new world order.

Nor is this a trivial and sentimental issue. God intends to create a new heaven and a new earth and everything that belongs in such an environment will be a part of it. God is going to re-fashion His fallen creation. The question about dogs (or any other creature for that matter), raises therefore another, and more important, question: *what kind of heaven are we expecting*? It is often suggested that the reason why dogs (or any other non-human life) are *not* in heaven is because they do not have souls. As we saw earlier, this line of reasoning is altogether misguided. It displays a Greek or Platonic understanding of soul rather than a biblical one. What distinguishes human beings from other life forms in the opening chapter of the Bible is not the possession (or lack of) *a soul*. It is the fact that human beings are made in the "image of God" (Gen. 1:27).

Take a passage like Isaiah 11:6–9:

> *The wolf shall dwell with the lamb,*
> *and the leopard shall lie down with the young goat,*
> *and the calf and the lion and the fattened calf together;*
> *and a little child shall lead them.*
> *The cow and the bear shall graze;*
> *their young shall lie down together;*
> *and the lion shall eat straw like the ox.*
> *The nursing child shall play over the hole of the cobra,*
> *and the weaned child shall put his hand on the adder's*
> *den.*

They shall not hurt or destroy
in all my holy mountain;
for the earth shall be full of the knowledge of the LORD
as the waters cover the sea.

Wolves and lambs, goats and leopards, lions and calves, children and snakes—are these merely metaphors of an anticipated better future? Is Isaiah merely giving us a picture of the coming rule and reign of the Messianic-King, a "child" and "son" upon whose shoulders the government shall rest, and whose name is "Wonderful Counselor, Mighty God, Everlasting Father, Prince of Peace" (cf. Isa. 9:6)?

Or is the prophet depicting the spread of Messiah's rule, as mainline *postmillennialists* believe? The metaphors of peaceful coexistence of wild animals then function as a way of describing the spread of the gospel across the world.

Or is Isaiah's portrait of a restored Eden meant to convey precisely what it says—a world in which the curse of sin is removed and God's creation exists in the harmony and peace of its original state? And if so, the new earth is going to be like the original creation, with all its variety of animals, birds and fish. If the new earth will have topography that will remind us of the Serengeti Plains, the English Cotswolds, or Rocky Mountain National Park, then will it not also include all its wildlife that currently inhabit these regions, including the Pyrenean Ibex, Caribbean Monk Seal and the Tasmanian Tiger, animals that are currently extinct?

Of course, there are questions:
- Will there be dinosaurs?
- Will animals eat vegetation rather than each other?
- Will snakes no longer bite?

And ten thousand other questions, most of which we cannot answer! But uncertainty about some of the details need not prevent us thinking about broader principles and expectations.

FOOD

In the next chapter, we will focus on *differences* between this world and the new earth. For now, let's ask questions about *continuity*. How will the new earth resemble the one we already know?

One area of continuity is biology and physiology. We will have resurrected *bodies*.

Take the matter of eating and drinking. Paul sees the resurrection of Jesus as a "model" for our own future resurrection: "Just as we have borne the image of the man of dust, we shall also bear the image of the man of heaven" (1 Cor. 15:49). Jesus' resurrection body is the "firstfruits" (1 Cor. 15:20). His current body is more than a guarantee of our future resurrection; it provides the *template* for our future body.

Jesus ate fish cooked on a charcoal fire in His resurrected body beside the Sea of Galilee (Luke 24:40–43; John 21:1–19). And whilst it may be true that further changes in Jesus' body take place from resurrected to ascended state, the Bible does not specifically say so. Can we therefore conjecture (and for now, conjecture is what it is) that our future existence will include eating? After all, the future form of the kingdom is described in terms of a banquet (Luke 14:16–24), or a wedding meal (Rev. 19:9). And, at the inauguration of the Lord's Supper, Jesus said, "I tell you I will not drink again of this fruit of the vine until that day when I drink it new with you in my Father's kingdom" (Matt. 26:29; Mark. 14:25).

And what about eating meat in the resurrected body, as Jesus did? Meat-eating is first mentioned *after* the flood (Gen. 9:3), suggesting to many that before the flood human beings were vegetarian. Should we therefore assume that in a redeemed universe, human beings will revert to a vegetarian diet? The logic seems flawed if we follow the example of Jesus after His resurrection. To some, the very thought of killing is wrong; but to others, killing for the sake of food is ethically justifiable. And *if* we follow the logic, will we hunt in the new world? Having never enjoyed the experience here, I find it difficult to imagine it there; but is it altogether out of the question? Will there really be "No Fishing" signs on every pool and lake and river? The logic gets complicated: how will the depletion of fish be remedied? In the next chapter, we will address the statement (by Jesus) about no marriage in heaven. And presumably, no sex. And therefore, no procreation. No babies will be born in the new earth. Will this also be true of animals and birds, and fish? Our minds begin to reel at the complexity of this line of thought.

Exploration and Inquiry

Perhaps a surer way to ask about the life to come is to ask the following: for what purpose was humankind created in the first place? The answer is found in the so-called "cultural mandate":

> *The LORD God took the man and put him in the garden of Eden to work it and keep it.* (Gen. 2:15)

As we hinted at earlier, not all creation was paradise. Humankind was given work to do, to subdue the earth and bring it under His lordship. Things have been made a million times worse because of the opposition and frustration that now manifests itself in creation. The ecological crisis is a result of sin. But even in paradise, Adam and Eve were to work to bring about order and beauty.

This might suggest that in the new heaven and earth, exploration and discovery will continue to be a feature of life—of eternal life, harnessing the universe for the glory of God. A host of related ideas are involved:

- Our minds will continue to expand as knowledge increases.
- The new heaven and new earth will not be a regress to primitive life, requiring the reinvention of the wheel or the discovery of DNA.
- Scientific and geographical exploration (to name but two disciplines) will continue to occupy our imagination and analytical inquisitiveness.

Will the discovery of information be easier in the new heaven and new earth? Perhaps. It is difficult to outline the effects of sin on the process of discovery and knowledge. The debilitating effects of memory loss, faulty reasoning and self-interest alone have catastrophic consequences on the process of discovery and investigation. Free from this contagion, what possibilities in advancement would there be? Is it not likely that God intends for us to discover and grow in our human advancement in the world to come rather than be given masses of information all at once?

What, for example, will the possibilities be for travel and exploration in the new heaven and new earth? To imagine that no such exploration will be possible or desirable is to stifle imagination and deny what is, after all, a God given mandate to humanity in Eden. We were made to ask questions and discover answers. We were created to admire beauty in art, music, literature and architecture, wherever beauty can be found.

Moreover we were made to create beauty, not just to admire it, as the early records of human beings demonstrate in the line of Jubal (musicians), Tubal-cain (metallurgy), Oholiab (embroidery) and Bezalel (carpentry) (Gen. 4:21–22; Exod. 37:1–5; 38:23). And if that was God's original purpose, why would it not continue to be His purpose in heaven? Music, art, architecture, design, literature—all of it and more. Songs to compose, books to write, buildings to construct, skills to develop.

Rule and Dominion

Exploration, discovery and creativity are all aspects of rule, exercising dominion over the created order. In the new heavens and new earth, Christians are going to reign with Christ. Writing to Timothy, Paul cited a trustworthy saying:

> *If we have died with him, we will also live with him;*
> *if we endure, we will also reign with him.*(2 Tim 2:11–12)

Just as Adam was told to exercise a kingly *dominion* over the original creation (Gen. 1:28), Christians in the new heaven and earth will also exercise dominion. They will reign over the new creation as vicegerents of the creator.

Elsewhere, Paul asks: "Do you not know that we are to judge angels? ..." (1 Cor. 6:3). What does this mean? Perhaps he meant that we will join in the condemnation of fallen angels, but the context suggests that Paul has in mind the holy angels. Since these angels have no sin, what possible judgment could there be? The Greek verb for judge (*krino*) also means to rule, or govern. Redeemed humanity, created and re-created in God's image (angels are not created in God's image), will rule over all creation, including God's exquisite angels. These splendid creatures are ministering spirits created to grant aid to human beings (Heb. 1:14; cf. Ps. 34:7; 91:11).

When the disciples asked an embarrassing question about greatness in the kingdom of God, Jesus responded:

You are those who have stayed with me in my trials, and I assign to you, as my Father assigned to me, a kingdom, that you may eat and drink at my table in my kingdom and sit on thrones judging the twelve tribes of Israel. (Luke. 22:28–30)

Eating, ruling, assessing. All this suggests we are to expect an extraordinary future.

We are, of course, only scratching the surface.

What no eye has seen, nor ear heard,
nor the heart of man imagined,
what God has prepared for those who love him.
(1 Cor. 2:9)

Chapter 7
Like the Angels

For in the resurrection they neither marry nor are given in marriage, but are like angels in heaven. (Matt. 22:30)

There will be no marriage in heaven. Jesus said so, explicitly.

The issue troubles us. Christians who enjoy a happy marriage find it hard to understand. It's not just sex, though it would be decidedly unbiblical to attribute anything unspiritual about sex. That is what got the medieval Roman Catholic church (via Augustine) into all sorts of trouble. It is the "no marriage" aspect that is most troubling. Life-long partners are friends, best friends. We share everything with them. And it is difficult to imagine the good life—the very *best* life—without such intimate, exclusive friendships. I once heard someone say, "Well, if we can't be married, can we at least share the same room?" I understand the sentiment.

And when you re-marry, for whatever reason, things get complicated. And there were some who asked Jesus about it.

John married Jane and quickly thereafter died. His brother Joe married Jane, but again, tragedy ensued and Joe died. Another brother, Jack married Jane and the misfortune occurred again and again when four more brothers, Jim, Jake, Jeff and Jordan married Jane and promptly died. Eventually Jane died, too. She had been married, in turn, to seven brothers. On the resurrection morning, assuming they were all Christians, who will Jane recognize as her husband?

The details of this strange tale are fantasy, but you may recognize that behind it lies a conundrum put to Jesus by certain Sadducees (Matt. 22:23–33). Their point was not to inquire about marriage so much as to ridicule the notion of a *bodily* resurrection where issues like this might arise. They asked the question in this way because Levirate law in the Old Testament required that a brother of the deceased husband marry a childless widow and raise up a family in the deceased brother's name. You may also remember that this is one of the issues that lies in the background of the story of Boaz and Ruth in the Old Testament—an important story because Jesus traces His own lineage to the fruit of this marriage!

A DIFFERENT EXISTENCE

The Sadducees did not believe in a physical resurrection. And that, as they say, is that. The question about the woman and her successive husbands was just a way of mocking the very idea of a physical existence after death. Souls can mingle without any such mess. And Jesus saw that there was a more important issue on the table. A physical resurrection *and* the issue of marriage in heaven.

In more ways than one, marriage ends at death. "Till death us do part," is a signal of the permanence of marriage in this life as well as a recognition of marital obligation on the death of one of the partners—allowing the living partner to remarry without the suspicion of bigamy.

I do not think that we should over-interpret this passage; in a way that suggests that we will not have close friends in the new heaven and earth. Jesus had close friends— Peter, James and John—and the latter was His closest friend. I see no reason to doubt that we shall experience these kinds of friendships in the new earth, and with those who have been our spouse and best friends here in the old earth. And perhaps this helps us understand a little Jesus' statement about marriage. It is not the intimacy as such that is dearest but the companionship and the love. And Jesus didn't say that we won't experience the friendship and the heady sense of love that two people know.

SHALL WE RECOGNIZE EACH OTHER?

Friendships and companionship require recognition. We shall know each other in heaven. True, Mary Magdalene, at first, did not recognize the resurrected Jesus, supposing Him to have been a gardener (John 20:15). And later that same day, Cleopas and his companion on the Emmaus Road failed to recognize Him despite what appears to have been a two-hour journey with Him in which He explained to them the Old Testament Scriptures. It was not only His face they did not recognize; they did not identify His voice. It was only later, in Emmaus, when they ate a meal together, that "... their eyes were opened, and they recognized him ..." (Luke 24:31).

Both instances contrast with other resurrection accounts where Jesus was immediately recognizable. This suggests that there are specific reasons for the seeming camouflage of Jesus' identity in these instances.

Take the case of Cleopas and his friend. Various explanations have been suggested: it was late afternoon and the sun was in their eyes (this does not explain why Jesus' voice would not have been familiar to them); their refusal to accept the earlier testimony of the women that Jesus was risen led them to close their minds as to the possibility that this was Jesus; they were in a state of shock, a "sad(ness)" clouded their minds (Luke 24:17).

None of these explanations are convincing. And Luke tells us himself that another explanation is needed. They were "prevented" from recognizing Him. Later, their eyes were "opened," but *initially* their eyes were "... kept from recognizing him" (Luke 24:16, 31). God (rather than Satan) kept Jesus' identity hidden. Why? Perhaps to prepare the disciples for a clearer understanding of Jesus' identity.

Earlier in his ministry, when speaking about His death, Luke made the comment, "But they did not understand this saying, and it was concealed from them, so that they might not perceive it ..." (Luke 9:45; cf. 18:34). When they did perceive Him, it was all the more delightful and glorious.

And Jesus *was* different from how they had seen Him before He died. The body He had before His crucifixion was capable of death. The one He now has can never die. What the two on the Emmaus Road saw, therefore, *was* different. As one author puts it, "The disciples were looking at the first, and so far the only, piece of incorruptible physicality."[1]

You're Bigger Than I Remember!

Have you ever had the experience of meeting someone you thought you knew, but there was something different about them? They had put on weight, or lost it. They were older, bent and no longer the spritely figure you recall from days past. Sadly, age and decay can make even those whom we thought we knew well appear different. In some instances, I have exclaimed in astonishment to my wife, "I barely recognized him!" This is what the Fall does to us.

Now consider the reverse. If, as Paul says, our "... momentary affliction is preparing for us an eternal weight of glory beyond all comparison" (2 Cor. 4:17), it

---

1   N. T. Wright, *Surprised by Hope: Rethinking Heaven, the Resurrection, and the Mission of the Church* (New York, NY: HarperOne, 2008), p. 160.

is hardly surprising then that the resurrection body will have a "glory" an appearance of significance, that will make us hard to recognize. I will still be "me" and you will still be "you." And as soon as this is perceived, there will never be any doubt as to who we are. But there will be a change—a change so magnificent that it will be difficult at first to make the connection. But as you think about it, this transformed, glorious "you" had been viewed before—in part, in glimpses, in shadow.

On one of my speaking engagements, a stranger came up to me and said, "you're bigger than I thought." Thinking of my fondness for bread and pastries, I shrank inside and wondered what was coming next. People say the strangest things! "Well, not bigger so much, as different." "Ah," I thought to myself, "that I can live with."

So will it be in the new heaven and new earth. People that we knew will be bigger—*different*, but still the same person that we knew in this world. Better. Greater in personality, affection, love, talent, patience and so much more.

There are going to be some things that will be the same as they appear to us right now. But there are also going to be differences.

BODIES FIT FOR A NEW EXISTENCE

Think, for example, of our resurrection bodies. How continuous will our future bodies be with the ones we have right now? This is a more complicated question than it first appears. Buried bodies, for example, decay and after a few hundred years, through excavation and building projects, even the skeletal remains are no longer intact. And what of those who are cremated? What happens to the bodies of, for example, the forty martyrs of Sevaste in the fourth century who bravely endured brutality and burning, and whose ashes were scattered in the fast-flowing river?

God can re-create our bodies so that in all important aspects they are our own. And yet, in equally important ways, they will be different. They will be bodies fit for a new existence and a new environment, one in which sin and death have no part.

This raises other questions:

- Will our bodies age?
- Will they change in any way?
- Will they grow tired and require sleep?
- Will we experience pain, if we fall on rocky ground, will they bleed?
- And what age will we be?
- Will we all look like athletes?

If we assume an ability to recognize one another, we must also assume that we will not all look alike. The original creation displayed variety and we should expect the new earth to do so too. Revelation 5:9 and 7:9 speak of "every tribe" present in the intermediate state. The new earth, therefore, will be populated with redeemed people with ethnic identities of skin color and other features that suggest national origin.

Overgrown and Emaciated

The perfection of the new heaven and earth requires that our bodies will be as God intends, without the distortion that comes from corruption and misuse. Our bodies will be both perfect and beautiful. But what does that mean? Augustine mused on this topic:

> [O]vergrown and emaciated persons need not fear that they shall be in heaven of such a figure as they would not be even in this world if they could help it ... [The body] shall be of that size which it either had attained or should have attained in the flower of its youth, and shall enjoy the beauty that arises from preserving symmetry and proportion in all its members.[2]

How "old" will our bodies appear to be? And what about children who die in infancy and those who never see life outside of their mother's womb? Will they appear as infants or adults? We are on the edge of speculation. Not that this has prevented some from giving an opinion. Thomas Aquinas, for example, argued that we will all be the age Jesus was when He was crucified:

> All will rise in the condition of perfect age, which is of thirty-two or thirty-three years. This is because all who were not yet arrived at this age, did not possess this perfect age, and

---

2   Augustine, *City of God*, 22:19, 22:20 *The Nicene and Post-Nicene Fathers*, First Series. Ed. Philip Schaff. 1886–1889. Volume 2 (14 vols.). Repr. (Peabody, MA: Hendrikson Publishers, 2004), p. 499.

the old had already lost it. Hence, youths and children will be given what they lack, and what the aged once had will be restored to them: "Until we all attain the unity of faith and of the knowledge of the Son of God, unto a perfect man, unto the measure of the age of the fullness of Christ."[3]

C. S. Lewis also had some interesting thoughts on this issue. In *The Great Divorce*, Lewis imagines (unhelpfully without any scriptural support, as it happens) someone in the "grey town" (hell or purgatory, depending on how long one stays there) catching a bus to the foothills of heaven. In the description of what he sees, there is the following:

The earth shook under their tread as their strong feet sank into the wet turf. A tiny haze and a sweet smell went up where they had crushed the grass and scattered the dew. Some were naked, some robed. But the naked ones did not seem less adorned, and the robes did not disguise in those who wore them the massive grandeur of muscle and the radiant smoothness of flesh ... no one in that company struck me as being of any particular age. One gets glimpses, even in our country, of that which is ageless—heavy thought in the face of an infant, and frolic childhood in that of a very old man. Here it was all like that.[4]

---

3   Thomas Aquinas, *The Catechetical Instructions of St. Thomas Aquinas*, Trans. Rev. Joseph B. Collins. The Eleventh Article, "The Resurrection of the Body," (Baltimore, MA: The Catholic Primer, 2004), p. 50.

4   C. S. Lewis, *The Great Divorce* (London, UK: Fontana Books, 1949), p. 29.

No one seemed of any particular age. Will deceased infants and children be adults in the new earth? Will mothers hold their infants in their arms and have the joy of watching them grow into adulthood, free from the effects of sin? The Lord is infinitely kind to His people. Perhaps He will allow us this kindness, too.

And what about relationships? Brothers and sisters, parents and children? Might it not be that God will allow us to relate to each other within the same relationships that we currently experience? Our children will always be our children and our parents will always be our parents. And husbands and wives will also know their common history and shared memories. Surely!

THE SAME, BUT DIFFERENT

But an abrupt discontinuity enters, too. Scripture is very clear that differences exist in the new earth. There is continuity and there is also discontinuity. Paul addresses this issue in his magnificent treatment of the resurrection body in 1 Corinthians 15:

> And what you sow is not the body that is to be, but a bare kernel, perhaps of wheat or of some other grain. But God gives it a body as he has chosen, and to each kind of seed its own body. For not all flesh is the same, but there is one kind for humans, another for animals, another for birds, and another for fish. There are heavenly bodies and earthly bodies, but the glory of the heavenly is of one kind, and the glory of the earthly is of another. There is one glory of the

> sun, and another glory of the moon, and another glory of
> the stars; for star differs from star in glory.
>
> So is it with the resurrection of the dead. What is sown
> is perishable; what is raised is imperishable. It is sown in
> dishonor; it is raised in glory. It is sown in weakness; it
> is raised in power. It is sown a natural body; it is raised
> a spiritual body. If there is a natural body, there is also
> a spiritual body. Thus it is written, "The first man Adam
> became a living being"; the last Adam became a life-giving
> spirit. (1 Cor. 15:37–45)

What kind of body can we expect in the resurrection? To
answer the question, he turns to nature. There are "hints"
in nature. When seeds die, flowers emerge. *Different* kinds
of seeds produce *different* kinds of flowers.

Now look at the heavens. What do you see? There are
different kinds of heavenly bodies—sun, moon, planets,
stars. And these heavenly bodies are clearly different from
anything we see on earth. They have a different "glory."
And, in verse 44, he provides a telling summary:

> The present body is "natural" (Greek: *psuchikon*)
> The resurrection body is "spiritual" (Greek: *pneumatikon*)

PRESENT BODY	FUTURE BODY
Perishable	Imperishable
Dishonorable	Honorable ("glory")
Weakness	Power

There are, as we have already said, aspects of continuity and discontinuity about the resurrection body. It is, in part, what the Westminster Confession is saying when it affirms that "the dead will be raised with the self-same bodies, and none other, although with different qualities."[5] What accounts for these "different qualities"?

THE RESURRECTION BODY IS "SPIRITUAL"

[The body] is sown a natural body; it is raised a spiritual body (1 Cor. 15:44).

What does Paul mean by saying that the resurrected body is *spiritual*? Several observations need to be made.

First, and this is very important, the use of the term *spiritual* to describe the nature of the resurrection body should not be viewed as a suggestion that the resurrection body is in some way non-corporeal. Paul is *not* suggesting that in the resurrection, we are bodyless spirits, or ghosts.

Equally disastrous is the conclusion that since the term *spiritual* is in contrast with the term *natural*, Paul intends to imply that the resurrection body is *un*-natural!

Jesus is the prototype of the resurrection body. Paul writes in Philippians 3:21 that God will "… transform our lowly body to be like his glorious body …" Similarly, here in 1 Corinthians 15:49, the apostle intimates that we will "bear the image of the man of heaven." Jesus' resurrection body bore the wounds of His crucifixion and consumed

---

5   *Westminster Confession of Faith*, 32:2.

food (from John 20:27 and Luke 24:36-43). Spiritual bodies must consider these crassly physical dimensions.

Paul's point, therefore, is not to undermine the biological nature of the resurrection body. Rather, his aim is to underline the powerful role of the Holy Spirit in resurrection life. Just as Jesus was declared to be the Son of God *"in power"* by His resurrection from the dead (Rom. 1:4), so in similar fashion, our body, currently weak and fragile, will be raised a Spirit-filled and Spirit-empowered body.

> *For [Christ] was crucified in weakness, but lives by the power of God … we also are weak in him, but … we will live with him by the power of God.* (2 Cor. 13:4)

We have little idea what this might mean for us. Perhaps an illustration might help. On many an occasion, I have spoken to people who suffer from sleep apnea. Deprivation of oxygen intake while they sleep causes them to become tired and weak. The prescription is typically a "sleep machine"—a device that enables a good intake of oxygen whilst sleeping. And the results are often dramatic. A new energy. A new life!

The Spirit-empowered and Spirit-gifted resurrection body will make our current bodies appear almost lifeless.

THE RESURRECTION BODY IS "GLORIOUS"

> *[The body] is sown in dishonor; it is raised in glory …* (1 Cor. 15:43)

The Scriptures provide us with a clue as to what this glory might be. At the transfiguration of Christ on the mountain, Peter saw Christ receiving *glory* from God (2 Pet. 1:17). John beheld His glory as of the only Son from the Father (John.1:14). There is a weightiness to the glory of Christ. The transfiguration was not a divinization of Jesus' body. But it was a glimpse of what the body of Jesus could become when freed from the weakness of this world. *Our* resurrection bodies will similarly bear a weightiness and significance, suited for the experience of seeing Christ "face to face" (1 Cor. 13:12).

I can hardly wait! It is going to be an adventure.

Postscript

Heaven is the Bible's word (in Greek and Hebrew) for "sky." It is one of the reasons why we tend to think of heaven as "up there." But, as we have seen in these pages, heaven is more nuanced than simply "above." The former physics student in me likes to think of it as a parallel universe. Heaven exists, *somewhere*. It is where the body of Jesus is right now. Heaven, in its current form, is a location in space: physical, tangible and real. Eventually, at the Second Coming, heaven is going to take the form of a renewed cosmos.

How then should we think about heaven?

Firstly, we should think of it (as heaven is right now and as it will be in its final form), a *perfect* place. Thinking of the final state of heaven for a minute, we should try and imagine life; *physical* and *mental* life without sin. Frankly, we have no experience of this, only vague anticipations of it. What is a mind free from the down-drag of sin capable of achieving? And what affections are possible when they are not wholly turned in upon ourselves. And is it possible, as a few resurrection incidents involving Jesus might seem to indicate, that the laws of physics as we now know them will be different in heaven? It is all too possible.

Secondly, we need to try and imagine a world without pain, disease and death. We questioned earlier whether pain as such will be absent. A central nervous system might require some basic forms of sensory perception even in a new earth. We will feel sharpness, roughness and softness. That the new body is incapable of bleeding seems to me to be a step too far. For my part, Jesus eating fish in a resurrected body seems to require more than we customarily think about when we try to imagine what heaven will be like: to begin with, a digestive system and all that goes along with it. The point is that it will be free from any notion of evil and whatever its precise form, it will be very good.

Thirdly, heaven is where we dream and grow and play and work along with all the redeemed saints. Whatever our occupation in heaven, there will be maximum satisfaction, enjoyment and pleasure, of the kind we have only glimpsed here and now. Laughter, accomplishment, fulfilment—being who we were made to be, achieving our full potential, and discovering a contentment that is wonderful (that is, full of *wonder*), is what heaven is about.

In its final form, heaven is a new earth. Mountains, oceans, rivers, lakes, forests, sandy beaches, birds, fish, animals of every kind.

And dogs. Sweet dogs to play and run with! All God's creation now restored. For us to explore and investigate and try to understand. That means science, and travel, and composition, and art, and music, and poetry; all that is pure and lovely and good. New talents to learn (I do hope so). New experiences to enjoy.

And all of it, forever and ever.

And the face of Jesus!

The greatest experience of heaven will be to gaze on Jesus' beautiful face. "They will see his face" (Rev. 22:4).

To look at Him with tears of joy and say, "Thank you, sweet Jesus. Thank you!"

And bow in worship and praise and adoration and sing His praises.

Christian Focus Publications

Our mission statement –

STAYING FAITHFUL

In dependence upon God we seek to impact the world through literature faithful to His infallible Word, the Bible. Our aim is to ensure that the Lord Jesus Christ is presented as the only hope to obtain forgiveness of sin, live a useful life and look forward to heaven with Him.

Our Books are published in four imprints:

CHRISTIAN
FOCUS

popular works including biographies, commentaries, basic doctrine and Christian living.

CHRISTIAN
HERITAGE

books representing some of the best material from the rich heritage of the church.

MENTOR

books written at a level suitable for Bible College and seminary students, pastors, and other serious readers. The imprint includes commentaries, doctrinal studies, examination of current issues and church history.

CF4•K

children's books for quality Bible teaching and for all age groups: Sunday school curriculum, puzzle and activity books; personal and family devotional titles, biographies and inspirational stories – Because you are never too young to know Jesus!

Christian Focus Publications Ltd,
Geanies House, Fearn, Ross-shire,
IV20 1TW, Scotland, United Kingdom.
www.christianfocus.com